To: Merrilee

God Bless You!

unlikely
angel

Ashley
Smith
Robinson

Prov. 3:5,6

ASHLEY SMITH

with Stacy Mattingly

unlikely angel

The Untold Story of the ATLANTA HOSTAGE HERO

WILLIAM MORROW
An Imprint of HarperCollins*Publishers*

ZONDERVAN, WILLIAM MORROW
Unlikely Angel

Requests for information should be addressed to:

Zondervan, 3900 *Sparks Dr. SE, Grand Rapids, Michigan 49546*

This edition: ISBN 9780310346623 (softcover)

Library of Congress Cataloging-in-Publication Data

Smith, Ashley, 1978-
Unlikely angel : the untold story of the Atlanta hostage hero / Ashley Smith with Stacy Mattingly.
p. cm.
ISBN-10: 0-310-27067-7
ISBN-13: 978-0-310-27067-6
1. Smith, Ashley, 1978- 2. Hostages—Georgia—Atlanta. 3. Violence—Religious aspects—Christianity. 4. Nichols, Brian. 5. Warren, Richard, 1954- Purpose-driven life. I. Stacy Mattingly. II. Title
BR1725.S49A3 2005
277.58'231083'092—dc22 2005020936

Acknowledgment is made for permission to reprint portions of The Purpose-Driven® Life by Rick Warren. Copyright © 2002 by Rick Warren. Used by permission of Zondervan.

Published in association with the literary agency of Calvin W. Edwards, 1220 Austin Glen Drive, Atlanta, Georgia 30338.

Some of the names in this book have been changed.

Article on page 16 of the photo insert: Copyright © 2005 by United Press International. Used by permission.

Photography credits
All insert photographs are courtesy of the author, except for:

Page 1 (top): Davis Turner/Getty Images; page 1 (bottom left): Splash News/NewsCom; page 1 (bottom right): Curtis Compton/NewsCom; page 12 (top): Davis Turner/Getty Images; page 12 (bottom): Davis Turner/Getty Images; page 13 (top): Davis Turner/Getty Images; page 13 (bottom): Tami Chappell/NewsCom; page 16: Parker Smith/Getty Images

Interior design by Michelle Espinoza

First printing July 2015 / Printed in the United States of America

For those who need hope
and don't know where to find it

author's note

The material in this book comes from my memory of the events and conversations related here. In particular, the hours I spent with Brian Nichols were extremely stressful; and while I have tried to remember events and conversations to the best of my ability, where I was unable to remember specific words, I tried to relate the substance of those events and conversations as best I could recall. Quotation marks are used in the book for readability, not as an indication that the words appearing in quotes are exact.

contents

1 hostage

Friday, March 11, 2005

At 9:45 p.m. my cell phone rang. I looked down at my caller ID—it was my step-dad calling from Augusta again. *What could he want this time?*

"What are you doing?" he asked.

I was exhausted, almost too tired to answer. I held the phone against my ear with my shoulder so I could carry a load of trash out of my second-floor apartment down to my car. I had been moving for two days. My new place was a smaller, bottom-level apartment on the other side of the complex. I didn't have much left to do here—just some vacuuming and painting to return the place to its original condition. But I wasn't doing any of that tonight. I needed sleep. I was driving to Dacula in the morning to see Paige.

"I'm moving the rest of my stuff," I said, trying to get down the stairs. *Just please let me get off this phone.*

"You're out? There's a man on the loose and you're out? Haven't you been watching the news like I told you?"

This was the second time my step-dad had called me about the guy on the news. The first time was late this morning when he woke me up calling. He kept talking about a man and shootings at the courthouse, and he told me to stay inside. I'd been up all night unpacking boxes, and I just didn't understand his concern. I mean, I lived in Duluth, maybe half an hour northeast of downtown Atlanta. "Thanks, but I'm not too worried about it," I had told him.

I learned a little more about the story when I went to work later in the day. I'd just started a second job at Barnacle's, a restaurant maybe five minutes from my apartment complex. The news was playing on the TV screens when I got there, and I caught the basics: A man had killed some people at the Fulton County Courthouse and now he was on the run. My coworkers were talking about it a lot, but I didn't pay too much attention. Being from Augusta, I was used to hearing about violent crime in Atlanta. And I had a lot on my mind with the move anyway.

"Look," I said to my step-dad now as I shut my car door and headed back up to the apartment, "this guy's not going to come after *me*. I mean, he could be anywhere."

I thought back to the five police officers who had come into Barnacle's for dinner. I was training to work the door, and as the men were walking out, I heard someone ask them, "Hey, have y'all caught that guy yet?"

"Oh, don't you worry about him," one officer said. "He's probably in Alabama by now."

I tried to reassure my step-dad: "You know, an officer who came into the restaurant said the guy's probably in Alabama, so I'll be fine. I've just gotten off work, and I have a few more things to get out of here. Then I'm done. I'll be on my way to the other apartment in a few minutes. I promise."

"Well, okay," my step-dad said. "Just get home and get inside and don't leave."

"Okay. Fine."

I loaded the rest of the trash into my car and drove the half mile or so to the other side of the apartment complex. I was thinking about what the next day would look like. I would see Paige in the morning. My Aunt Kim, who had custody of her right now, had brought her the two and a half hours from Augusta, and they were staying with my Uncle David's family in Dacula, about thirty miles northeast of Atlanta toward Athens. We were all meeting up at Uncle David's church at ten o'clock for a kids' ministry Olympics day.

Then I would work a day shift at Express in Gwinnett Place Mall and a night shift at Barnacle's. It would be a full day, and I felt completely shot right now. I knew I just had to get to bed. I couldn't let myself do any more unpacking tonight. Maybe one or two boxes, but that was it. *Really, Ashley, you can't get sucked into this.*

I pulled up to my new apartment and parked right in front of the door. I didn't have far to carry my things, only ten or twelve steps up the walk. When I got inside, I pulled off my gray knit work shirt and black leather belt, which left me in a white tank top and a pair of baggy jeans. Then I turned on the TV in the living room.

"Okay," I said, looking at the five or six boxes lined up in the middle of the floor. "Just one or two."

While the news played in the background, I began unpacking the boxes and putting things where they belonged. The eight-by-ten photograph of Paige holding that red flower could go on top of my stereo speaker near the door. The two gold angel candleholders could sit on my picture table for now—I was going to hang them on either side of that mirror propped up on the back of the sofa.

Now and then as I worked I heard what the news anchors were saying: The man from the courthouse was still at large. He'd killed three people. There was something about a green Honda. I didn't hear much. Mainly, I was focused on getting my house the way I liked it. I knew exactly where I wanted things—photographs, candles, lamps, books, knickknacks—and I just kept going.

At about eleven I stopped and smoked a couple of cigarettes. I only had one left in the pack now, but I purposely had not gone by the store after work to buy any more because I knew I was going to make it an early night. Looking around the apartment, I changed my plan just a little. I saw I was knocking out the boxes pretty quickly, and I thought, "I could be done with this really soon and be able to see Paige tomorrow, go to work, come home, and not have to worry with this anymore. I can finish. I really can."

I kept working until all of the boxes were empty, setting out the last couple of chunky candles on my picture table in front of the two living room windows. Then I stacked up the empty boxes right behind the front door. I had done it. I was ahead of the game. It was after midnight, but I was finished. I smoked my last cigarette and began to get ready for bed.

And yet I couldn't quite seem to make it to bed. I tried to wash clothes, only to find the washing machine in my laundry room wasn't hooked up right—when I threw in a few shirts and some detergent and turned it on, the machine just spewed water everywhere. After that, I kept straightening and rearranging picture frames and knickknacks. My perfectionist streak was suddenly in high gear, and getting things in place like I wanted them ended up being a huge job. Before I knew it, it was going on 2:00 a.m. I was still awake. And now I was out of cigarettes.

Too wound up to go to sleep at this point, and really needing to smoke—I always smoked right before bed—I decided to make a run to the QuikTrip, a mile or two from the apartment complex. It was chilly out, so I put on a long, hooded beige sweater and a tan knit cap. Pulling the hood up over my head, I grabbed my pocketbook and keys, opened the door, and went out into the night.

As soon as I stepped outside, I heard a rumbling noise. Glancing in the direction of the sound, I saw a large, dark blue pickup truck backing into a parking space at the end of the row to my right, maybe fifty yards away. I didn't think much of it. It was Friday night, and I'd been known to come in later than this. Plus, I'd just moved into this place; I figured the driver was probably a neighbor. I got into my car, backed out, and drove past the truck, rounding the corner to the stop sign. Looking over, I could just barely make out the driver's outline in the front seat.

About five or six minutes later I pulled into the QuikTrip parking lot on Satellite Boulevard. Right then I realized I needed to reset the clock on my dash. My battery had died the night before while I was moving. This car was basically on its last leg—it was an '89 Pontiac Bonneville with more than 200,000 miles. An Augusta friend had bought it for me the previous summer because it had air-conditioning, which meant I could drive my daughter, Paige, around in it when I visited her in Augusta at Aunt Kim's.

But I had only driven Paige in the car once. That particular day, Aunt Kim told me to drive Paige straight to her soccer game and back. This was the first time she had let me take my daughter anywhere in a long time—and I broke the rules. I stopped somewhere else with Paige, and I lost my privileges.

Now my car had begun to cut off in traffic—the engine would just sputter and go out and I'd have to crank it up, praying for it to start again. The battery had flat-out died for the first time the day before, when I was moving into my new apartment. I had loaded the car down with a bunch of my stuff and even hoisted my mattress and box springs onto the roof. Things were sticking out of the windows and trunk; the car was almost touching the ground. When it wouldn't start, I called someone I knew to come jump it and help me move a few heavy items over to the new place. I only had two friends in Atlanta, and they were not very close friends.

Bending down now to look at my clock in the QuikTrip parking lot, I thought, "That time's not right." I wasn't wearing my watch, so I took out my cell phone. It was right at two o'clock. I punched in the correct time on the dash and ran into the store for a box of Marlboro Light Menthols. Then I got back on Satellite Boulevard and headed for home.

As I pulled up the short hill to my new apartment and took the sharp corner to the left, I noticed the blue truck had moved. *Okay, what? What's up with this?* Now the truck was backed into a parking space directly behind where I had originally parked; and it was one space over from a free-standing garage, which meant I could only see the hood. Driving slowly toward my parking space, I got a better view of the windshield and tried to look inside. *Oh, God—help me. Someone's still in there.*

I had no idea what to do right then. The driver was just sitting there looking straight ahead. *Is he looking at my car? Looking at me?* I could feel myself starting to sweat. I knew this wasn't right. *Maybe I could just make a U-turn and drive off.* But where would I go? My mom lived nearby, but she and I had been fighting—I didn't want to go to her place, especially not at two in the morning. And I didn't have close friends in the area. Checking out the short distance between my parking space and the front door, I thought maybe I could make a run for it.

Okay, if he tries to follow me, I can just try to beat him to the front door, get inside, and lock it. I was starting to shake, sitting there in the car. Was this a stupid idea? *Ashley, think! Are you sure you want to try this?* I didn't really know what else to do at this point. *Just why'd you have to go out in the first place? Stupid cigarettes.* Trembling, I pulled the car into my space and shut off the ignition. *I guess I'm going for it.* I got my keys ready and reached for the door handle.

As soon as I stepped out of the car and shut my door, I heard a clicking sound—it was the truck's door closing behind me. *That's the driver.*

I was walking quickly toward the apartment now. *Just a few steps up this walk right here.* I turned my head slightly to check behind me, and I could see out of the corner of my eye a black man coming right for me. I could hear his footsteps, hear him getting closer. *Maybe he'll pass me and go to the stairwell.* I kept moving. Finally to the door, I got my keys in the lock, turned the knob, and pushed the door open. Then he was on me.

"Aah! Aah! Aah!" I was standing on the sidewalk, screaming at the top of my lungs.

He had me by the arm. There was a gun in my face. My pocketbook slid off my shoulder and crashed to the ground.

"Shut up!" he said in a harsh whisper. "Stop screaming! If you stop screaming, I won't hurt you. Just shut up! Shut up!"

"Don't hurt me! Please don't hurt me!" I could almost hear the gun firing. I braced myself. *This is it. Paige.*

Wrenching my arm, he got behind me, wrapped his arms around my upper body, and shoved me inside the apartment, pressing the gun into my side. The door bounced against the empty boxes I had stacked behind it, and I slouched in his arms, hoping that if he tried to shoot, I could somehow dodge the bullet by slumping to the ground.

Once he got me inside the small foyer, he closed the door behind us and locked it. I stumbled and stood up. My beige sweater had gotten pulled off and was now at my feet. *Just get me out of here alive, God. If he rapes me, so be it. Just let me make it out of here. Let me see Paige again. Please!*

The man was waving the gun in my face. "Why'd you scream?"

I was backed up against the closet door directly opposite the front door and standing about two feet away from him. He had a baseball hat pulled low over his face. I looked down and saw one of his pant legs was rolled up, exposing what looked like another gun tucked into his black sneaker.

"Please don't kill me, please don't do this. Don't hurt me. My little girl doesn't have a daddy and if you kill me she won't have a mommy, either. Please don't hurt me." I stuck my hands out in front of me, pleading. "My little girl . . ."

"Just calm down, quit moving. Don't do that. Just, I'm not going to hurt you if you just listen to me and don't scream again. Do *not* scream again, because if your neighbors heard you scream, then the police are on the way, and I'm going to have to hold you hostage and kill you and probably kill them and myself."

"Okay, okay, okay." The gun was about a foot from my face.

"Why'd you scream?" he asked again. The pitch of his voice rose. He was glaring at me from under that hat.

"What? Why did I scream? I . . . I don't know you. It's two in the morning. You have a gun pointed at me. I'm scared!" My voice was breaking now. *Oh, God, just get me out of this.*

"Is anybody here with you?"

"No, I'm by myself. I just moved in here. Please don't hurt me."

"Your little girl—where is she?"

"She's somewhere else. I'm supposed to see her in the morning." *Just thank you she's not here.*

"Okay," he said. "Now, do as I say and walk to the bathroom."

Shaking so hard I could hardly get air, I moved slowly off the closet door as he said and began to walk.

2 do you know who i am?

With this guy on my heels, I stepped out of the small foyer and began walking across the living room toward the back of the apartment. I could feel the floor vibrate with his footsteps. I had left the overhead light on in the kitchen when I went out, and it was shining over the bar that separated the kitchen and living room; but I still struggled to get my bearings in a place I'd only lived in for two days. I stumbled over Paige's massive toy box sitting out in the middle of the floor. I must have lost my clogs somewhere coming inside, because underneath my feet I was feeling the stiff rug in front of the sofa. I thought, "This is it. He's going to shoot me in the bathroom and leave me there so he won't have to see my face."

Making my way toward the extra-wide door—this must've been a "handicapped" apartment—leading to the back hallway, I kept hearing the gun going off in my mind. The guy was right behind me now, right up on me. I could see his black sneakers just behind my legs when I looked down at the floor. I felt my body tensing up as I walked. I imagined my step-dad's annoying refrain of the past year: "Atlanta's a bad city, and something bad could happen to you there." Then I saw Paige's face. I was supposed to see her in the morning at Uncle David's church. *What's Aunt Kim going to tell her now? Her heart will be shattered. I won't even get to tell her goodbye. Just like Mack. Just like Mack.*

Right then I could picture the scene from four years ago when Mack died. I could see the lights on the police cars flashing around that dark parking lot in the apartment complex just a mile or so from where we lived. Mack was in the ambulance now. Those people who hurt him had all run off. The police were questioning some others near an apartment building, and I wanted to get to the ambulance so I could climb inside with my husband. He had that horrible wound near his shoulder. His eyes were closed. He wasn't breathing.

"Give him some more air!" I had screamed earlier as the paramedics worked on him. But nothing was happening. He wasn't responding. "Breathe!"

As I was trying to figure out what to do, an EMT worker approached me. "Mrs. Smith," he said. "How long have y'all been married?"

"Two and a half years," I said. I just wanted to go over there to the ambulance.

"We're sorry," he said. "He's gone."

"Gone? What do you mean?" I asked, not understanding. "Where'd he go?"

My husband was dead at twenty-three. Murdered right near our house, just a few hours before dawn. It wasn't supposed to happen. He couldn't even speak at the end, couldn't tell me he loved me. Nothing. He didn't even get to say goodbye to Paige.

I got to the small hallway in the back right-hand corner of the living room and made a left into the bathroom. Feeling for the switch on the wall, I turned on the overhead light. A small lamp sitting on the bathroom counter was already on. I walked directly across the room and stood in the corner of the L-shaped countertop with my back to the mirrors that lined the adjoining walls behind me and to my right.

Now I was facing this guy. Just to my right was a long stretch of empty counter space with the lamp at the end and a tall linen cabinet.

To my left was the sink and, next to it, a burgundy candle and a framed picture of Paige and me from my cousin's recent wedding. Paige was dressed all in white; she was the flower girl.

He stood several feet away, directly across from me in the doorway, pointing the gun.

For the first time I could focus on what he was wearing—a big red down jacket, black dress pants, and the red baseball hat still pulled down low over his face. Trying desperately to remember every detail about him just in case I made it out of this place alive, I made a mental note that he was several inches taller than me—I was looking up at him—and in the thick jacket, his arms and shoulders looked huge, like those of a weight lifter. I couldn't get a good look at his face under the hat. Defined jaw, prominent chin—I could see that much. I could tell he was pretty dark-skinned. I could see his eyes shifting from one side of the bathroom to the other. But the rest of his face was hidden. I guessed he was probably in his thirties.

"I've got to hear if the police are coming," he said, still speaking in an angry whisper. He turned his head to the left and stepped back into the dark hallway, listening. His body disappeared in the shadows, and I could hear his down jacket swish as he moved. All I could see in the light now were his red sleeve, his hand, and the gun.

Standing there, I started to feel totally sick about Paige—just imagining what she would have to go through if this guy killed me right here. She had lost her daddy. He was never coming back. What was it going to feel like now for her to lose me too? *She's going to question you, God. She'll ask, "Why'd you take my mommy and my daddy away? Why did you leave me alone?" What are you going to say to her? How are you going to make this up to her? I know my child's heart, and it's going to break.*

I was remembering the first time I saw Paige after labor and delivery. I was sitting in a hospital bed looking at a Polaroid that one of the nurses had brought in to me. Paige was just two pounds fourteen and a half ounces, and she was so fragile when she was born, the nurses had to take her away before I even got to look at her. But there she was in that photograph, so tiny and all wrapped up in those tubes and begging for her life. It just about killed me. When I finally saw her hooked up to those machines in the special-care nursery, I felt as if my heart was coming apart right there. "Let her be a fighter," I was praying. "Just let her be a fighter. Let her make it." And she did make it. She was perfectly healthy. *My miracle baby. My angel child. I've got to make it out of here for her.*

Moving my small vanity stool aside with my foot now, I pushed myself up and sat on the bathroom counter, trying to get control of my thoughts. He was still standing in the doorway with the gun. I was shaking profusely. My chest, neck, and arms flushed with heat, and I could feel sweat beading above my upper lip. How was I being mugged right now in my own home? If this had happened two days ago, I wouldn't even be in this apartment. If my grandparents hadn't agreed to loan me that money at the beginning of the week, I would never even have moved in here. But then, thinking about the last four years of my life—Mack's murder, my descent into that drug addiction nightmare, giving custody of Paige to Aunt Kim, the car accident, all of it—I thought, "Why am I surprised? Of course I'm being mugged in my own home. Of course this is happening to me."

"Do you know who I am?" He had stepped back into the light and was shifting slowly from one foot to the other, speaking in a low, angry tone, his jacket swishing. He looked massive—his body almost filled the doorframe. And he kept that gun pointed at my chest.

"No," I said, squinting at him, trying to read his face. *What does he mean—do I know him? This is Atlanta. I'm being mugged in the middle of the night. How am I supposed to know who he is?*

Then he asked, "Have you been watching the news today?" He kind of cocked his head back, exposing more of his face, and under his hat I could see he was looking me dead in the eye.

"A little," I answered, still confused. I grasped the countertop with my hands and leaned forward. What was he getting at?

"The whole courthouse thing?" he said. "You know, *Bri-an Nichols*?" He pronounced the name slowly, his voice getting louder but still low and controlled.

"Ye–yes," I said, starting to understand. *Is it him?* I strained to better make out his features. I hadn't paid much attention to the mug shot on TV. Plus, I'd been at work and dealing with the move all day. I couldn't remember that guy's face. *Could it be? No. Was Brian Nichols even the guy's name? This couldn't be happening to me. Not after everything else. Surely not after everything else. Not this guy. He's supposed to be in Alabama. The officer said Alabama.*

He took a step toward me and was standing fully in the light now. Still pointing the gun with one hand, he raised his free hand and grasped the bill of his hat. Then in one quick motion he ripped off the hat, took another step toward me, and stuck out his neck, almost getting up in my face.

"*Now* do you know who I am?" His voice was louder and angrier. He froze in front of me with his face stuck out in this terrifying expression and his eyes wide open, as if he were waiting for me to feel the full impact of his identity.

I leaned back toward the mirror, trying to pull away from him. My hands and arms were trembling uncontrollably at my sides. "Uh-huh, yes," I said, nodding slowly. "I know who you are." *Three people. This guy killed three people. At the courthouse. He was loose and now he's here? In my apartment?* I struggled to understand. Was this happening?

Now I could see his face in full view. His head was closely shaven, nearly bald; his forehead was high, his cheeks filled out, and his eyes small and kind of set back under his brow. He looked younger than I thought—maybe in his early thirties, not much older than me. He was dark-skinned, but his complexion looked washed out. His eyes were shifting again from one side of the bathroom to the other. He looked angry, frustrated, almost afraid.

"Please, please don't hurt me," I pleaded, sitting up straight and clasping my hands together to keep them from shaking. "Please don't hurt me. I have a five-year-old little girl and she needs me." I could feel the blood rushing to my face, and I was having trouble getting air. "My husband died. She needs me. Please."

In that moment I could picture Mack again, stretched out in the parking lot of that apartment complex with the paramedics' machine hooked up to him. "Give more air," the machine kept saying. "Breathe. Give more air. Breathe. Give more air."

"Give him some more air!" I cried out. "Help him breathe!"

Suddenly Brian Nichols moved back toward the bathroom door. Still facing me, he stepped out into the hallway and turned his head to the left toward the living room again.

I wiped my palms on my jeans. *Does he hear something? Surely somebody heard me scream. I was screaming bloody murder out there. Somebody had to have heard me. But what if they did? I'm stuck in here with this guy who's already killed a bunch of people and he's got a gun on me. I don't want to die in a shoot-out.*

I remembered an expression Mack's mother used to say: "Expect the worst and be pleasantly surprised." If I could just stay alive, I thought. *Whatever it takes, God. Whatever it takes.*

"Look," Brian Nichols said forcefully. "The police could already be on their way." He stepped into the bathroom, eyeing the shower curtain across the room to my left.

"Get in the bathtub," he said, motioning toward the tub with his head. "Get in the bathtub now."

3 seeing pain

Get in the bathtub?" I asked, hesitating. *Oh, man, that's the last thing I want to do.* The bathtub would be the place where he could blow my brains out and make the least mess. He could just shoot me, close the shower curtain, and leave.

I looked to my left at the yellow-green-and-blue plaid shower curtain I had just put up the day before. I was thinking that it didn't match anything else in this bathroom. My mind was tripping out so much from all the stress, I started thinking about the decor in here—how I wanted to get away from the burgundy-and-gold theme of my bathroom in the other apartment. I really wanted to go for a fresh, summery look in here, more like that shower curtain.

"Get in," Brian Nichols answered in the same low, controlled tone. He stood there pointing that black handgun and waiting for me to move. I slid off the counter, walked to the tub, pushed the shower curtain back, and stepped in.

"Sit down," he said.

I sat down like he asked, feeling my stomach turn as I crossed my legs Indian-style and heard my socks slide over the plastic tub. My back was against the side of the tub so that I could face the room. Brian Nichols was standing in the doorway, which was now on my left. The toilet was just to my right. The long, empty counter was just across the room on the far wall, and the sink was on the right-hand wall just past the toilet.

Sitting there, I suddenly thought that maybe all of this was God's will. I mean, what if it really was God's will for me to die tonight? What if I was supposed to just die right here in this bathtub, another victim of the guy my step-dad had warned me about? It looked like it was going to happen. Brian Nichols could shoot me right here. And maybe God was ready for me. Maybe he was going to take me home now because I couldn't get my life together, just like Aunt Kim had prayed after I gave her custody of Paige two years ago. Aunt Kim told me what she'd prayed: "Lord, if Ashley isn't going to quit doing those drugs, then just take her home."

I thought back to the phone calls I had made over the last several months to the guy here in Atlanta who could get me the drugs. I would only call every now and then. Maybe once a week, if that. I was getting it together now. I was getting back on my feet. I could stop when I wanted, I would tell myself. But sometimes when I dialed the guy's number I would pray, "Lord, let him be there, just this one last time." Or, if I was feeling really guilty, "Lord, let him *not* be there. Don't ever let me be in touch with him again. Help me." All of the back and forth. *Lord, let him be there. Lord, let him not be there.* Months of it. What was I doing? I was playing with God. I was mocking him. Maybe now he was saying, "It's over, little girl. You can't stop, so I'm going to have to bring you home."

I felt a wave of heat sweep over my body and my heart start to race. *God, if I've done something that's going to make you take me away and leave Paige without a mother, please, please forgive me. I won't do those drugs anymore. Just give me another chance. Give me a chance to get it right. I really do want to live for you. I want to see Paige grow up. I want to be there. Don't let her miss out because of my mistakes.*

Then I felt a sickening sense of dread. It was probably too late now. Too late for second chances. Too late for me to get it right. Actions had consequences—I had already learned that. And my actions spoke for themselves. I had shown God I really couldn't put those drugs down, and maybe tonight I was going to have to pay for it. Maybe in God's eyes it would be best for Paige if he just took me off the scene completely. Maybe I didn't deserve to see her grow up. *Please! If I could just go back, I would change so much. I understand now. I want to change!*

But I couldn't go back. I couldn't change anything. I had made my mistakes—all of that was over. It was done. I was sitting here in my bathtub with a gun in my face, and I was in God's hands. That was all. I was just going to have to fight for my life tonight and trust God to do his will. There was nothing else I could do.

Brian Nichols was still standing near the door.

"Look," I said, trying to sit up straight against the side of the tub. "I told you, my husband died. Somebody stabbed him, and he died in my arms four years ago. Now my little girl doesn't have a daddy. I can't leave her without a mommy too. I can't leave her alone like that. Please! She needs me to live. Just please don't hurt me."

The tears started coming, and I struggled to get my words out. *I can't leave her without a mommy too. I can't leave her alone.* I could see Paige's face in front of me again. Those full cheeks, fair skin, and little pug nose. She looked just like Mack.

"What'd you do, spit her out?" I had asked Mack once when we were standing over Paige's incubator at the hospital. She stayed in the special-care nursery for six weeks after she was born before we could take her home. Even with all of the machines and tubes hooked up to her, anyone could see that she looked like her daddy.

Mack was almost too scared to touch her. He had never held a baby before, let alone one so little and sick. The first time the nurse asked him if he wanted to hold Paige, he said, "No way!" and took a big step back.

"Look, son," the nurse replied firmly, "if you don't hold her, I'm gonna drop her." Mack threw out his arms instantly and took Paige, and his heart was won.

I nudged him and smiled. "Tried to get out of that one, huh?"

Keeping the gun pointed at me, Brian Nichols turned his head toward the living room and set the baseball hat, still in his hand, down on the counter next to the small gold lamp. "My husband *died*," I said again, putting my hands on the side of the tub and choking on the tears now. "Somebody *stabbed* him. My little girl won't have anybody if you hurt me."

I wasn't sure if he could hear a word I was saying. He was looking around the bathroom again. His eyes shifted to the sink, the toilet, the floor, the toilet, then back to me; and even then, he wasn't looking me in the eye. *Does he even see me? How can I get him to feel what I'm feeling? He's got to get this.* I needed him to think about what Paige would have to go through if he killed her mother, to imagine what it must be like for a little girl to know that someone had also killed her daddy. *My husband died in my arms. They stabbed him to death, and he was gone. Gone, they said.*

Now my mind was back in that dark parking lot the night Mack died. I could see him hanging onto the passenger door of the truck, putting his foot on the footboard as if he was going to get in. Standing several yards away, I could tell right then that something was wrong. He couldn't even lift himself into the truck. His body just seemed to crumple.

"Mack!" I called out, running toward him. When I got there he collapsed in my arms and his eyes closed almost instantly.

"Honey, what's wrong? What's wrong?" I said, sinking to the ground with him. "Honey? What *is* it, what's *wrong*?"

But he didn't answer. He didn't open his eyes. Then I looked down and saw his white tee shirt turning red around the front of his shoulder. "Help me! Please!" I cried out. "Please! Somebody help me!"

Brian Nichols waited a few seconds, then walked across the bathroom and took a seat on my vanity stool near the sink. I had picked up that stool at an Augusta flea market, polished the gold metal frame, and covered the cushion with striped silk to match the burgundy-and-gold stripes I painted on the walls in my old bathroom. Why was I thinking about this decor stuff again? My mind was all over the place. I remembered it took me two weeks—what felt like forever—to paint those stripes on the walls. I didn't own a yardstick and had to measure and draw the lines using a ruler. And I wanted the lines to be perfectly straight.

Maybe that was my step-dad's doing. Maybe my perfectionism all went back to those hours of chores he gave me to do every Saturday during high school. I couldn't even go off to the lake with my friends because I had pages of chores front and back. Not just chores like "Clean the bathroom," but "Get up on the counter, remove the light fixtures, wipe down every lightbulb, and get into every corner." Week after week of that kind of work just changed me. I mean, I gained some discipline and all. But now I was a twenty-six-year-old woman who drew perfectly straight lines on the walls of a large bathroom using a pencil and a twelve-inch ruler.

Letting the gun droop in his hand, Brian Nichols sat opposite me several feet away from the tub. He was leaning forward with his forearms propped on his knees and the big red jacket riding up behind him. The vanity stool had basically disappeared underneath his body. Hunched over the delicate, gold-plated frame, he reminded me of a teenager trying to ride a little kid's bike. In the mirror behind him, I could see the back of his shaved head moving as he talked.

"Do you know what I was on trial for?" he asked, looking down at me.

"No," I said. "I don't know why you were on trial." All I knew was that he had killed those three people at the courthouse.

"Well, let me tell you this: I was falsely accused. My girlfriend of seven years falsely accused me of rape." He was looking just to the left of my head as he talked, as if his mind was somewhere else. *Rape? Oh, God, protect me in here*. I glanced down, and where his pant legs were riding up, I could see that other gun—what looked like a small black gun—tucked inside his black sneaker against the inside of his right leg. He wasn't wearing any socks.

"Falsely accused you of rape?" I said. "That's terrible. Man, I'm sorry you had to go through that. And being on trial and everything. I can imagine how awful that was. Nobody should have to go through all that. I'm really sorry." At this point I was going to agree with everything he said and try to feel his feelings—whatever it took to connect with him and gain his trust. He had to see that he could relate to me.

"I mean, she really did me wrong," he continued, the pitch of his voice rising. "She went out with our minister. Can you believe that? What kind of woman do you think that is?" He sat up and raised his left hand in the air—for emphasis, I guessed—and with his right hand he held onto the gun. Now he was squinting intensely and looking me in the eye.

"I'm sorry," I said. "With your minister? That's horrible. She had no right to do that. That's just wrong. That was your minister. What a terrible thing to do. I'm sure you *were* falsely accused." I was prepared to start calling this woman every name in the book if necessary.

Then he said, "You know, I did her wrong too. I got this other girl pregnant. But I tried to apologize, and she went out with one of our ministers. Can you believe she did that to me? I mean, we were supposed to be in church." He leaned back suddenly, then sighed and came forward again, propping his elbows on his knees.

"No," I said, shaking my head. "I can't believe she did that."

I was thinking about his religious background and how I might be able to use it to relate to him. But I was also looking into his eyes right then and noticing something. For a brief second I thought I saw something real. Whatever really happened with his girlfriend, I was seeing something in his eyes behind the anger and frustration—something that made him look like a lonely, hurt little boy. His heart really did seem broken, and I knew I was seeing a flash of real pain.

If I could just learn more about what I was seeing and relate to him there, I thought, then maybe I would have a chance. Maybe I could actually make it out of this apartment alive. Maybe I would get to see Paige in the morning. *Help me, God. Help me do it. I know what it's like to hurt. Please just help me find a way in.*

4 trying to relate

Do you know what it's like to be in jail?" Now his voice was low again. He sat leaning over his knees with his head bent down. "I mean, do you know what it's like *being* in there? A girl like you—you've gotta have no idea." He looked totally disgusted.

"Okay," I thought, "I know I can use this. I can use my own experience. I can use Mack." *Lord, help me do this right. Help me show this guy that I understand.*

"Yes," I said, answering in a low tone to match his. "Actually, I do know." He looked up at me with his brow lowered a little and his head turned to the side. I wasn't sure if he believed me, so I just started talking.

"I've actually been in jail myself several times. Mostly for DUI-related stuff, but also for shoplifting and possession, and battery once against my step-dad—but all that got resolved and he and I are fine now.

"Most of the time I stayed in a holding cell until someone came and picked me up, but I did go upstairs to the women's floor in population a couple of times. And I hated it—just the way they treat you up there. I mean, they talk to you like you're stupid. They throw that orange jumpsuit at you like, 'Here! Put this on!' They give you a hard time if you want to use the phone. Just ordering you around like you're a piece of crap. And the food is nasty.

"The longest I stayed in jail was, I think, maybe twenty-eight hours or so, but my husband—he was locked up for a week or two on a DUI, and he said it was a lot worse on the men's floor. He told me they just treated him like crap; he didn't even feel human. So I can just imagine what you've been going through."

Brian Nichols watched me as I talked. I was rambling on, and he had that distant look in his eye again. Studying his face for a minute, I tried to imagine what an Atlanta prison would be like for someone on trial for rape. It had to be rough. Being locked up, period, was rough.

I remembered what it felt like sitting in that holding cell at the Richmond County jail after being arrested for the first time. It was the summer after my high school graduation, and I had just turned eighteen. The cops had picked me up for shoplifting in the parking lot outside Macy's at Augusta Mall. Two Tommy Hilfiger shirts were stuffed into my pocketbook; I had stolen them for a friend, a small-time drug dealer, who in return was going to give me some cocaine. Outrunning the security guard in the store, I thought I could make it outside with the shirts, but by the time I busted through the side door into the parking lot, the cops were already there waiting on me. The friends who were with me fled the scene in my car.

I waited for a while in the holding cell, declining my one phone call and expecting one of my friends to drive my car to the jail and pick me up. The holding cell was just a ten-by-ten concrete room, and it was overcrowded that afternoon. I was packed in there with about six other women, most of them messed up on drugs and right off the street, all talking about what they were in there for—prostitution, selling drugs, possession. There was a toilet in the corner and a bench against one of the walls. I stayed quiet, trying to play it cool, but I was pretty scared.

I must have looked like the preppy high school girl I had been for most of my teenage years. My long, light brown hair was styled and curled under. I wore nice clothes and gold jewelry. I was tan and physically fit from years of playing basketball. But underneath all that, I was starting to become someone else. I'd gotten hooked up with this bad crowd of people at the end of high school—I'd moved on from my pot-smoking high school friends to the people who could actually get me the drugs, and this crowd was into harder stuff like cocaine. I was just getting a glimpse of the world those women in the cell were talking about—the drug world—and I liked the way the drugs made me feel so much, I didn't really stop to think about what might happen to me if I kept going. It never crossed my mind that I might end up like those women—that I might turn into one of them. But that's pretty much what happened.

Looking at Brian Nichols sitting on that vanity stool across my bathroom—seeing the blank, just totally miserable look in his eyes—I remembered how alone I felt sitting there in that holding cell waiting on my one friend to come. Hours went by and he never showed up, and I ended up having to call my grandparents. I was living with them at the time, and I was scared to death to make that call. A former marine, my grandpa was a tough man. He had helped raise me and was my primary father figure all through my growing-up years. My own daddy wasn't around; I had only seen him a handful of times. Mema and Papa took care of me when my mom worked late, and they gave me anything I wanted—the Plymouth Laser my friends had driven off in at Macy's was a gift to me from them.

Now I was going to have to call my grandparents from jail—not that I thought they would be surprised exactly. They knew I was running with a bad crowd. They knew I was doing drugs. I was only living with them because my mom and step-dad—who married when I was eleven—had thrown me out of their house right after graduation. I had been rude and disrespectful; I was coming home late at night high. My mom and step-dad didn't want me setting that kind of example for their two younger children, and they hoped Mema and Papa could straighten me out.

But I was rude and disrespectful to my grandparents too. I would go to work at Red Lobster, where I waited tables, and then stay out all night drinking, smoking pot, or doing cocaine with my friends. Most nights I came home drunk or high. I yelled at my grandparents.

I found every excuse not to show up Sundays at their church. They tried to use tough love—Papa took my car away too many times to count—but I didn't care. The harder my grandparents were with me, the harder I got with them. When I finally called them from the Richmond County jail and asked them to come and get me, they told me I could just sit my butt down and stay there.

Right now, sitting in my bathtub at gunpoint, looking across the room at Brian Nichols and trying to find a way to connect with him, I could almost feel that same wave of pure misery and loneliness I felt when I hung up the phone in jail knowing Mema and Papa were washing their hands of me right then. The guards gave me that orange jumpsuit and some nasty, flimsy, white Velcro shoes that I was afraid would give me foot fungus, and they moved me upstairs. All of the cells were full, so I was handed a blue mat and told to go lie down in an open space near a big Plexiglas window.

As darkness came on, from the window I could see the lights at the Red Lobster where I worked—the restaurant was just across the street. I was scheduled to work a dinner shift that night, and I wondered what everyone must have thought when I didn't show up. If they only knew I was here, right across the road, locked up and looking at those lights while they served dinner. What would they think? But only a few people knew where I was that night. And they had left me to myself. I was on my own, lying on a hard floor with a bunch of messed-up strangers, facing a long night and a loneliness that I didn't know how to fill.

"Well, my girlfriend put me in there," Brian Nichols started again. Now I saw the anger return. He was squinting, looking to the side of my head, and the pitch of his voice rose. "She put me in jail. And now I'm a soldier for my people. My people needed me for a job. And I'm doing it. Those people did my people wrong."

What in the world? What does he mean—soldier for his people? Does he mean race? People of his race? He wasn't making sense. This was not a good sign. If I could keep talking to him and maintain a conversation and feel his feelings, then I might have a chance. But if I couldn't understand him, reason with him, or get through to him, then I was in trouble. I looked at the gun—it was a pretty large handgun—still in his hand. I looked at his face. His eyes were shifting around the bathroom. *What can I say right now, God? What can I say to bring him back down?*

Then he asked, "Have you ever shot a gun before?"

"Yes," I said calmly. My legs were starting to cramp up in the tub, but I didn't want him to know. I kept sitting Indian-style and looked him in the eye. "I was eighteen, I think, and I shot a little .22 once in the backyard with my boyfriend." I didn't know what he was getting at with this question. Maybe he wanted to figure out if I was a threat to him—if I would be capable of using his own gun if given the chance. I watched him now, expecting him to continue, but he didn't; he just sat there, still hunched over on the stool.

I wondered if I *could* use his gun. It looked a lot like a large automatic handgun that one of my boyfriends after Mack's death used to carry. Guns were a big deal in the drug scene, and all the guys I knew owned at least one. This particular boyfriend had several, and I never wanted them around. I hated guns. They scared me. They could go off anywhere. This boyfriend always kept one under the passenger seat in his car, and whenever we went anywhere I worried. What if the gun went off under me? What if we got into a car wreck and it went off and I died that way? I just didn't like guns at all.

Brian Nichols kept quiet. He was looking around now, and I wasn't sure what to do to get the conversation back on track. Behind him on the counter to his right I could make out the photograph of Paige and me in that gold frame next to the sink. I could remember that picture being taken. Paige and I were standing outside the sanctuary in the church where my cousin Sarah got married back in December. I wore a black evening dress and long blond extensions in my hair that were flipping out over my shoulders and driving me crazy. Paige wore her beautiful flower girl's dress—lots of white fabric down to her ankles, a petticoat, and sheer white sleeves—and she had her long blond hair pulled back. I was leaning forward slightly in the picture so that I could hug Paige in close.

I thought about those weeks and months after Mack died—how I had lived on Xanax and pain pills and just totally checked out on Paige. One batch of pills would wear off and I would take another handful, sometimes as many as thirty pills a day. I cooked for Paige. I took her to her church school. But I didn't give her any real love and attention, and I know she suffered. Every time I had the chance to leave the house, I did. Babysitters would come over and Paige would cry. "Mommy will be back later," I would say as I ran out the door to go get high on something—pot, ecstasy, more Xanax; ecstasy *and* Xanax. My attitude was "Y'all take care of her, she's not my problem. Y'all take care of her. I don't want to feel anything."

Now, waiting for Brian Nichols to say something, I thought, "Why did I have to fall so far? Why couldn't I get myself together after Mack died? I couldn't even stop those drugs for Paige. I just abandoned her for all that. And now she has to pay for it. It's not fair. Aunt Kim's done a great job, but Paige is my child. I've got to do better so I can get her back." *God, you know I want to do better. I'm trying so hard. I'm fighting to get there. Please don't take me away from her now.*

I pushed my hair back from my face and readjusted myself in the tub. I knew there was no way I could leave my daughter on this earth without a parent. I just couldn't do that to her. She didn't get to say goodbye to her daddy, and I wasn't going to leave her the same way. I was just going to have to make it to my uncle's church in the morning. There was no other option. *I have to do it, God. You've got to help me find a way.*

I focused back on Brian Nichols. He was sitting on that stool looking at the floor, running his hand over his bald head. He was thinking. But about what? What could I do to relate to this man? What could I say to make him see me as a person just like him? I had to get back in the game.

"What's your name?" he asked suddenly.

Should I tell him my name? Yes, I should tell him. Any question he asks, I need to answer simply and honestly. "Ashley," I said.

Then he stood up. I saw the vanity stool wobble underneath him. It was missing a knob on the bottom of one of its legs, and I could hear the metal rattling on the linoleum. He pulled his jacket down at the waist and stepped forward onto my orange shag rug in the middle of the floor. He was towering over me now, and he aimed the gun at my chest. I sat up as straight as I could in the tub. *God, hold him back. Don't let him lose it. Don't let him shoot.*

He said, "Ashley, I don't feel comfortable with you."

"Okay," I said. "Please don't hurt me." I knew I had to get him to feel comfortable. If I couldn't do that, I wouldn't make it. *What can I do differently? What do I do here?*

"You're going to have to sit right there for a minute and not move."

"Okay, I won't move." I sat in the tub, barely breathing, not wanting to do anything to set him off.

Then he looked toward the hallway to his right. "Because if you move," he said, "I'm going to have to hurt you."

5 i want to relax

He looked down at the orange rug, inhaled deeply through his mouth, and kept talking. "Because then I'll have to hurt you and I really don't want to do that right now. I don't want to hurt anybody else. I just want to relax. I've had a long day, and I don't want—I just want to chill out. I want to relax. So right now I'm going to walk around your house to get the feel of it and get comfortable."

"Okay," I said, wrapping my arms around myself to try and keep from trembling in the tub.

His eyes shifted as he talked, and he used his hand—the one not holding the gun—to express himself. To me he looked exhausted. I wondered where he'd been all day and how many hours he'd been on the run. Without my watch I had no idea what time it was now, but I figured this guy had been running for a while.

I knew what it felt like not being able to relax. I thought back to that long night of driving around the streets of Augusta before my mom and Aunt Kim finally checked me into the mental hospital. That was almost two years ago now. I was driving around all night strung out on ice—also known as crystal methamphetamine, the drug I was using basically around the clock by then—and I had been awake for days. My paranoia was in full force, and I thought terrorists were tracking me through a chip in my cell phone. I thought the terrorists were sending me subliminal messages through the songs on the radio, trying to lead me somewhere.

Near daybreak I finally got to Stevens Creek Road, the road I would take to get to Aunt Kim's subdivision. That's where I thought the terrorists were leading me—to her house—but I kept driving back and forth on that same road as if I couldn't get off. Back and forth. Back and forth. Messed up out of my mind. I couldn't have been driving more than half a mile each way. I would drive in one direction, then turn around and go back the other direction. Back and forth. Back and forth. I kept thinking I was going the wrong way.

Brian Nichols turned and walked out of the bathroom now. I sat up as straight as I could in the tub and looked to the right, trying to watch him in the mirror over the sink, which faced the door. In the mirror I could see that he had walked right across the hallway and into my bedroom at the front of the apartment. There was no overhead light in my room, but the double doors to the closet—on the left-hand side as you walked in—were open, and the bright closet light was still on as I had left it when I went out for cigarettes. In that light I could see Brian Nichols go straight to the two windows, which faced the street, and look out, separating the blinds.

What's he going to do to me if the cops show up? I know somebody must've heard that scream—the people next door, the people right above me, somebody. The walls are so thin in this place, there's no way they didn't hear me. I remembered what he said when he first got in the door: "If the police come, I'm going to have to hold you hostage and kill you, kill them, and probably kill myself." I didn't know what to pray—let the cops come, don't let the cops come?

Between the two windows where he was watching the street stood a white, waist-high chest of drawers. I had painted it six months ago, along with my taller dresser and two nightstands, and spray-painted the hardware slate gray. All of the furniture—what used to be the spare room furniture in my old, larger apartment—looked fresh and brand new, and it matched the full-size, white canopy bed that I was using now as a four-poster bed without the canopy. My comforter, pillow cases, and dust ruffle were white too. I was planning to paint the walls a summer green; the can of paint was sitting in the far right corner of the room next to my TV stand.

On top of the small dresser next to Brian Nichols was my big, brown wicker basket of important books. I could see him going through the books now. He would look through the blinds at the street, then go back to the books, then look through the blinds again. I hoped he was paying attention to those books and learning a little bit about who I was. My Bible was in there—the big, black leather study Bible that my grandpa gave to me for my first Christmas. My name was in gold lettering on the front: Elizabeth Ashley Copeland. I needed this guy to look at that Bible and think of me as someone who went to church like he did.

Then there was my Alcoholics Anonymous book, which I had used in my three-month recovery program the year before; I had put silver sticker letters across the top of the navy, hardback cover to read "1 day at a time." Paige's Bible was in the basket too, along with my journals and quote books and a book called *Why a Daughter Needs a Dad. Just let him keep thinking about Paige. Let him remember what I said—he can't leave her without a mommy too.*

I was remembering what Mack said to me in the car that day I picked him up from work and told him I was pregnant with Paige. I told him I had good news and bad news. The good news was that I had just gotten a new job. The bad news—I called it bad news because I knew it would be bad to him—was that I was seven weeks pregnant. Mack and I weren't married then. I was twenty and he was twenty-one, and we were living with his parents in their trailer out in the country. He figured out the "bad" news without my having to say it and just flew off the handle sitting there in my car. "You can have an abortion or you can leave!" he yelled. "Have an abortion or get out of my house!"

I knew Mack's anger, his moodiness, but I also knew where I stood. And I was not going to budge on having my baby. Looking into his eyes, I answered calmly. "Okay then. Bye. See ya. I don't believe in abortion and I'll never do that. God gave me this baby and I'm having it. I can raise it on my own if I have to. I don't need you, and I sure don't need your help."

In the bathroom mirror now I could see Brian Nichols still going through my books and looking through the blinds. I knew he had to have picked up my copy of *The Purpose-Driven Life* sitting right there on top with my Bible. I was almost done with that book. I was doing my chapter-a-day every morning—I was giving God his time like I promised, even if it meant I was late for work. If nothing else happened, I was going to hear God speak something to me every day. That's what I told Aunt Kim. I was trying to show her, my mom, my grandparents, and everybody that I was doing better now. I was going to be Paige's mom. I could raise her on my own just like I told Mack. I was going to make it—I really was this time.

I could still picture myself sitting in Aunt Kim's church in Augusta the day I got my *Purpose-Driven Life* book just a month earlier. Aunt Kim and Paige were sitting in the very front of the school auditorium where the church met; I was visiting Paige that weekend and came into the service late. As I took a seat in the back, the pastor started talking about how the church was going to start *The Purpose-Driven Life* study. If anybody wanted the book, he said, we could just grab one on the way out—even if you didn't have money, you could take one. All I had in my pocketbook was a dollar bill that I had rolled up and used to snort some ice. I sat there in my seat and I said to myself, "You know what, I'm going to give this dollar bill in the offering—this is going to be my drugs going in the offering plate for that book. That's what I'm going to do. I'm turning it over to God."

In the bathroom mirror, I watched Brian Nichols turn away from the basket of books finally and walk over to my tall dresser, which was up against the right-hand wall and opposite the bed. Sitting on that dresser were a mirror, my jewelry box, and a picture of Paige in a silver frame outlined with pink stones. That was a recent picture—Paige was sitting on a rock in a photographer's studio, wearing white Capri pants. Everywhere Brian Nichols went in this apartment he was going to see my little girl. *Lord, let it click in his mind—this is a child who needs me. Let him see her. Let him really see her.*

He stood there for a minute, opening and closing the drawers—all I kept in that dresser were clothes—and then he walked out of the room, taking a left into the living room, his down jacket swishing as he walked.

"Ashley, are you okay in there?" he called out as he walked by the bathroom.

How weird. Is he actually checking on me, or just making sure I'm not trying to pull something in here? "Uh-huh, yes," I said.

No longer able to see him in the mirror, I just listened. I could hear him going through drawers in my kitchen, which was on the far side of the apartment and separated from the living-dining area by the thin bar that was about chest-high and lined with framed photographs of Paige and my family. The kitchen was totally unpacked now. I had only been moving for two days, but I had been working at it for most of that time. I had taken off the last few nights from school—I was studying to be a medical assistant so I could get out of waiting tables and make a stable income for Paige and me. And I had snorted a little bit of ice when I was moving stuff out of my other apartment so I would be able to stay up for long hours. Just last night I had stayed up working on this place until dawn.

What's he looking for? I kept hearing drawers open and close, cabinets open and close, utensils bang together. He already had a gun—did he want a knife? *Please, not a knife.* Right then I remembered the coroner's call after Mack died: "Your husband was stabbed to death with a knife." "A knife?" I asked, totally in shock. "He was stabbed to death? I never saw a knife."

Brian Nichols was still making noise, obviously looking for something specific. I had put everything in its place, so it couldn't be that hard for him to find what he wanted. I hated not being able to find things. If I went to look for something and it wasn't where it was supposed to be, it just made me crazy. Mack was the same way. He was deep into keeping things in order—and keeping the house in order was my job. If he came home from a long day at work and was looking for something, and it wasn't there, I would hear, "Honey, where's it at? It's supposed to be here." Then the slamming of drawers or cabinets or closet doors.

"Do you have a cell phone?" Brian Nichols was calling out to me from the kitchen now.

"Yes," I answered. I just had a cell phone, no landline.

"Where is it?"

"In my pocketbook." I had no idea where he would find my pocketbook—a fake Louis Vuitton bag Aunt Kim had just given to me for Christmas. I dropped it somewhere coming in. Wait. Now I remembered. "It might be outside on the sidewalk," I said.

I was still trying to be as helpful and cooperative as possible. He said he wanted to relax. He said he didn't want to hurt me. But he said he *would* hurt me if he had to. If I could just do what he asked and stay relaxed myself, then maybe he would feel that he could finally chill out. Somehow I had to make him feel at ease. I had to find a way to gain his trust. I looked across the bathroom now at the picture of Paige and me on the counter, and I could feel the tears come up. *My angel child. My baby. She needs me, God! I've just got to make it out of here to see her in the morning.*

Hearing him walk toward the hallway, I sat up to look in the mirror over the sink again. I could see him coming—he had taken off the red jacket—and as he entered the bathroom, I turned my head away from the mirror so I could watch him walk through the door. Now I saw he was wearing a black blazer that matched his black dress pants. He glanced over at me, then went straight to the counter to put down what he had brought with him: the gun—no knife, thankfully; my cigarettes (*I guess he found my pocketbook*); a small, glass ashtray from off the coffee table; some masking tape he must have gotten from my kitchen drawer near the stove (*is that going over my mouth?*); and a two-liter bottle of raspberry soda I had just bought at the grocery store. "Well," I thought, "make yourself at home, dude—whatever you need to do."

Then he walked over to the toilet to my right, closed the lid, and set down one of my brown extension cords (*he's been in the laundry room)* and a long, cream-colored panel of fabric from my living room curtain set. I didn't like the looks of that cord at all. *Is he going to strangle me with that?* I could almost feel my throat tighten, feel the plastic against my neck. I had no idea what the curtain could be for, but I didn't like it. For some reason I didn't like those two things sitting off to the side by themselves.

When he turned around and faced me, I saw he was bare-chested underneath his blazer. His pecs were rippling in between the black lapels; and seeing where the jacket seams hit his shoulders, I could tell just how broad those shoulders really were. *I know I'm in good shape, but man, if this guy comes at me, I'll never have a chance trying to fight him off. Just don't let it come down to that, God. This guy could really, really hurt me.*

"Here's the deal," he said. For the first time he had put the gun down; it was lying on the counter next to the masking tape. "I want to relax."

I nodded. "Okay."

Then he picked up the bottle of raspberry soda and pointed it at me the way he had been pointing the gun. "Want something to drink?"

"No," I said. *He's pointing a bottle at me now and offering refreshments. Is this a good sign?*

"Do you want something to eat?"

"No." I tried to read his face. *Is he calming down?* "No," I said again, eyeing my cigarettes on the counter, "but I would like a cigarette."

A cigarette sounded really great to me right now. How long had it been since I smoked? Had I smoked one coming back from the QuikTrip? I couldn't even remember. Probably so, because I had really needed a cigarette when I left the house. Looking at the pack in his hand, I saw that it was open, so, yes, I had smoked a cigarette sometime after 2:00 a.m. I still had no idea what time it was now.

Setting the bottle of soda on the counter, he took out a cigarette, stepped toward the tub, and handed it to me. Then he pulled out a lighter I didn't recognize. I only used Bic lighters; they were fat with colored shells. This was one of those slim, transparent lighters—you could see the fluid inside—and the shell was pink. I wasn't sure where it came from. Maybe he found it in one of my end-table drawers in the living room. Maybe it was his.

As I put the cigarette to my mouth, he bent down over me and held out the lighter. I moved the cigarette to the flame and inhaled deeply, looking at his large hand in front of my face and wondering if I was going to see blood on it. *I don't think I can handle the sight of blood right now, God.* Focusing on the inhale, I closed my eyes and sat back against the side of the tub, then let the smoke out slowly through my mouth.

He stood up, took out another cigarette, and lit it for himself. Then he set the ashtray down on the side of the tub.

For a few seconds he said nothing. He took a couple of drags. He reached for the soda bottle and cracked it open. I could hear the fizz. He took a swig or two.

"Look," he said then, blowing smoke out of his mouth. "I don't trust you. I want to relax for a minute, and I can't relax with you like that, so I'm going to have to tie you up."

I put out my cigarette in the ashtray and sat up straight. This was not good at all. He could tie me up and rape me. He could tie me up and kill me. *God, this is really bad—you've got to do something to help me.* I couldn't let him tie me up, no questions asked. Not with the stakes this high. I had to at least say something.

Putting my hands on my knees, I looked up at him like he had just hurt my feelings. I was being so helpful, so cooperative. I had just been sitting here enjoying a cigarette for a minute. I wasn't trying to fight him or make his night miserable. I was all for him relaxing. My house was his house. *Can't you see I'm trying to be your friend, dude?*

Then, with all of that feeling in my eyes—squinting and lowering my brow like the most confused person in the world—I asked him, "Why?"

6 tied up

"Just stand up," he said.

No explanation. Just stand up? Okay, I guess I'll stand up then.

I stood up in the bathtub and shook the cramps out of my legs. He put out his cigarette, moved the ashtray to the counter, and picked up the roll of masking tape. Then he stepped toward me.

"Please," I said looking up at him, "just—just don't hurt me, okay? I can't leave my little girl. Please."

I decided I was going to keep mentioning Paige until I was blue in the face. I didn't care how sick and tired he got of hearing about her. She was my focus. She was all I cared about. He was just going to have to hear about her until I got it through his head that I could not—that I would not—leave my little girl alone without a mommy or a daddy.

"Turn around," he said.

I sure didn't want to turn around. I did what he said, but I did it slowly—and I kept my face turned to the side so I could watch him out of the corner of my eye. Standing there in the tub facing the wall, I started to fear he was going to throw the extension cord over my head and strangle me. I turned my head around even further toward the toilet where that cord was lying. My thought was, "If that thing's going around my neck, then at least I want to see it coming."

"Put your hands behind your back."

I followed instructions. I put my hands behind my back and crossed them at the wrists, palms up, over my tailbone.

"No," he said, "not like that—in a praying position."

Okay, God. He wants my hands in a praying position, so I'm praying right now. Please—please protect me, Jesus. Only you know where this is going and what I need to do. I'm not ready to go home yet. If you want to take me, I trust you, but I'm not ready. Oh, Lord, I'm just not ready.

I couldn't put my palms together behind my back unless I bent my arms and positioned my hands at my lower back—or really forced my arms down and pushed my chest up, and that posture strained my shoulders. I went with the bent arms, and as soon as my palms were touching, I heard the strip of masking tape buzzing off the roll.

I felt him start the tape on my wrists—holding the end in place with his hand—and then bring the roll under my hands so that it touched my lower back, and back over; under and over, working the tape down my hands toward my fingers. Then I felt something give and heard the roll of tape hit the side of the tub and finally the floor.

"What kind of tape is this, anyway?" he asked, groaning and bending down to pick up the roll. I guessed the tape had broken while he was wrapping. *What do you mean, "what kind of tape is it"? Obviously it's masking tape, dude.*

"Masking tape," I said. I was trying to remain calm, do what he asked, and answer all of his questions. He pulled the end of the tape off the roll again and started wrapping until my hands were taped up tight, forcing my shoulders forward a little.

"All right," he said, stepping to the toilet to grab the curtain and the extension cord. *Not that extension cord. Please don't let him use that on me.* "Now come in here."

I turned around and stepped out of the bathtub. I saw he was walking across the hall toward the bedroom. Then I thought of his girlfriend. *This could not be good. God, if he rapes me in there, what can I do? I can't put up anything close to a real fight taped up like this.*

I remembered something I heard once: "There's one thing worse than being raped, and that's being killed."

Okay, if he rapes me, I can deal with it later. I can survive it. I know I can. But just don't let him kill me. Let me make it out of here alive. Seeing Paige—that's the bottom line.

Walking toward the bathroom door, I noticed his red baseball hat sitting on the counter near the gold lamp. It was a nice-looking, brand-new Georgia Bulldogs hat. I loved the Bulldogs; all through high school I had watched Georgia Bulldogs football with my step-dad.

"Nice hat you got there," I said now, trying to be as friendly and casual as I could. He was standing directly across the hallway in my bedroom, between my tall dresser and the foot of my bed. *If I can just make some kind of connection, something real and human, then maybe I can convince him not to do whatever he's got planned.*

But he didn't answer. He just stood there looking really big in that black suit with his chest showing. In the light from my closet, his face looked blank; I couldn't read any emotion in his eyes. The curtain and that extension cord lay at his feet, and he was still holding the roll of masking tape.

I walked toward him, seeing his red jacket thrown on a small bench I had set against the wall in the hallway. And as I crossed into the bedroom, I went back to my old line: "Please don't hurt me," I pleaded.

"Sit on the bed," he told me. He motioned toward the foot of the bed. *All right, God, here we go. I'm in your hands here.* My big, white down comforter made the mattress look like a cloud.

I sat down right on the edge, and suddenly, facing him with my arms behind my back, I became extremely conscious of what I was wearing. Without my sweater, I was not well covered at all. Not even close to well covered. My jeans, bought when I was a little heavier—I called them my "fat jeans"—were hanging low on my hips, and my white thong underwear was showing. My white tank top—there really was very little to it; it was more like a camisole with a built-in bra—was not even long enough to cover my waist. Originally I had been wearing these clothes in the privacy of my home to unpack boxes. But now

I was afraid. *What is he thinking, looking at me like this? Am I getting this guy worked up?*

"Stick out your legs," he said. *Okay, I'm doing it. He left that gun in there on the counter. I know my legs are strong and I could kick the crap out of him if I had to.* I remembered all those days of weight training for basketball season in the Lakeside High School gym in Augusta with my Uncle David. Leg strength was critical to my game, he told me, and I spent all kinds of time on that squat machine.

I stuck my legs straight out in front of me now like Brian Nichols said, squeezing my thighs together. He pulled the strip of masking tape off the roll and, bending down over my legs, started the end of the tape on one of my thighs about midway up from my knees. Then he began to work the roll over and under my legs.

So he's taping my legs together? Okay. At least he's not going to rape me right now. I looked down at the extension cord lying to his right on the beige carpet. That cord was what scared me.

He was really close to my body now. His head was maybe a foot from my chest; his upper body was right over my legs; and his hands, working the roll of tape down my legs, were just inches from my knees. I could feel my legs begin to droop toward the floor a little. He kept working the roll, wrapping the tape around my shins, and finally stopped about midway to my ankles.

As he tore off the tape, I looked at the extension cord again. *What can I do? My arms aren't free. My legs aren't free. My knees won't bend. I can bend at the hips though. I could swing my legs from the hips.*

Dropping the roll of tape on the floor, he reached for the cord. *Okay. He's got that cord now.* I inhaled deeply, trying to get ready. He stood up and shook the cord out, holding it in one hand and untangling it with the other. Then he bent over me again.

What's he doing? He moved for my legs. *Thank you, God.* Grasping the cord with both hands, he placed it over my thighs. Then he crossed the ends underneath my legs and brought them up, crossed the ends over my legs and circled them under, working the cord down my legs that way until he got to the point where the masking tape stopped. Then he made several knots to tie off the cord.

"Is that too tight?" he asked.

That's bizarre. What kind of criminal asks if he's tying you up too tight? "No," I answered. The cord was tight, but not cutting off all of my circulation.

Next he reached down and picked up the curtain panel, that long piece of cream-colored fabric he'd gotten off my living room floor. He stepped toward me—so close I could feel his breath on my shoulder—and put the curtain around my back, holding both ends in front of me. He crossed the ends of the material in front of my body and then behind my body—doing that a couple of times—covering my stomach and arms and securing my arms at my sides. Finally he tied the curtain off at my side in a couple of knots. I couldn't tell what he thought the curtain would accomplish for him, considering my hands were already taped up pretty good, but I wasn't about to ask him.

He stepped back and looked at me for a second, checking out the job he had just done tying me up. I tried to scoot up on the bed a little higher, pushing myself up with my feet. "Satisfied?" I wanted to ask.

Then he said, "Hey, I really want to smoke some pot. Do you have any marijuana?"

What? He's just tied me up and now he's asking me for drugs? That's totally insane. I was just stunned, blown away. I mean, I had told him about being in jail. I'd mentioned that one possession charge. I guessed he thought there was a good chance I would have drugs in the house. *But come on! I'm this guy's hostage here. I'm freakin' tied up and he wants to get high?*

"No," I answered.

Suddenly I had an idea—something that I thought might win me some favor with Brian Nichols and just get him away from me, or at least get him focused on something else. Maybe with this I could really get him to see me as someone here to cooperate, someone on his side. I had to get him to let me out of this apartment. I was supposed to see Paige in the morning. The words came out the minute I thought them.

"No," I said. "Sorry, I don't have any pot. But I've got something else."

"Well, what is it?" He clasped his hands together and looked me in the eye, raising his eyebrows.

I glanced at the floor, then went ahead and threw it out there as if I were offering him a choice of soft drinks. "I've got some ice."

7 answering straight

I shuddered at those words. "I've got some ice." *Did I just say that? Ashley, what are you* doing? *What were you thinking? You idiot! I can't give this guy ice. He's just killed three people. What if it makes him as crazy and paranoid as it makes me? I've got to get out of this. God, help me find a way out. That was a huge, huge mistake. What did I just do?*

"Ice?" he asked. "What's ice?"

He doesn't know? He's been in jail and doesn't know? His question gave me a little hope. Maybe he would be afraid of the stuff. Maybe he wouldn't want it.

"It's meth," I said, looking down at the extension cord twisted around my legs.

"Yeah, I've heard about that," he said. "Do you smoke it?"

"You don't have to." I was still looking down.

I remembered being at a friend's house right when I started dating John. Mack had been gone about a year and a half. I had just moved out of our house because I couldn't pay the rent anymore. Paige was already living with Aunt Kim. I had only been using ice for a couple of months, but I was into it full force. "Where's my line?" was the first question of my day. And that was assuming I went to bed. Usually I stayed up on ice three or four days at a time. I lived that way for an entire year.

"I'm not having a girlfriend who smokes," John said to me. We were sitting in a room with some guys who were smoking the drug right then. They were using a glass bong with Kool-Aid or some kind of flavored drink at the bottom instead of water to make the stuff taste better.

"Look," I told John, "we're going to do ice either way. What difference does it make if I snort it or smoke it? Besides, you're smoking."

"It makes a difference," he said. "My girlfriend's not smoking." He didn't want his girlfriend to be thought of as a "crackhead."

I really was not up for getting into all of this with Brian Nichols right now—I didn't want to explain the different ways you could do ice. *Can't we just move on? How can I change the subject?* But I was the one who had put the whole ice thing out there. I had offered it. So I was just going to have to answer his questions straight.

"You don't have to smoke it," I continued. "You can hot rail it or snort it."

I wondered if Brian Nichols even knew what hot railing was. Not that it mattered. I didn't have any hot-railing tools anymore. I had given that method up after my recovery program last year. And I was thanking God for it now. The last thing I needed was Brian Nichols hot railing in my house and flipping out on me.

I started hot railing ice around the time I was seeing John. If he wasn't going to let me smoke, then at least I could hot rail and get the same effect. I would put the ice into a thin glass tube about three inches long and heat the bottom with a butane lighter until the tiny crystals turned to smoke. Then I would put the tube up my nose and inhale, and the drug would go straight to my brain.

I would feel the lift in seconds. Suddenly I was alert and exploding with energy, ready to start getting things done. The first time I ever tried the drug I was like, "Wow! This is great! I've been depressed all this time over Mack, and now I feel alive again—like I'm really somebody!" But then the paranoia would set in. I thought surveillance cameras were hidden in my house. I thought the police had set up a secret monitoring station in the dark blue van parked across the street. I thought terrorists were sending signals to each other through the air-conditioning vents. I would just lose my mind—it was all so real to me.

Eventually I got to the point where I was hot railing every four hours or so—usually a nickel-size amount of the drug that would last most people an entire day. I did it at my house or at friends' houses. For months I would spend several nights a week hot railing at the house of the woman who got us the drugs—it was a small, run-down place on a hill above a two-lane road outside of town. We called it "the crack house." I would come home not having slept and as crazy as ever, thinking people could read my mind, and I would ask myself, "Why? Why are you doing this to yourself? You'll never be fit to be Paige's mother like this."

My roommate, who didn't use ice, was so freaked out by how much of it I was doing that she took my hot-railing tools one afternoon when I was gone and threw them away. "You can't stop me!" I yelled when I got home and discovered the bag of tools wasn't at the top of my closet. "I'll just go out and get more!" I was strung out, paranoid, and miserable, but I thought I would rather die than quit doing that drug—and I almost did.

Brian Nichols began to nod. "That'll be good," he said. "That sounds like what I need."

I was still looking at my taped-up legs. *Okay, God, I'm in your hands on this one. I guess I'll just have to pay the price for whatever happens.*

"But first," he went on, putting his hands to the buttons of his blazer, "I'm going to take a shower and relax." He unbuttoned the blazer and took it off, hanging it on the left-hand post at the foot of my four-poster bed. *Well, at least that gives me a little more time.*

Glancing up at him without a shirt on, I thought, "This guy is huge. I guess they really do work out in jail." He looked like a linebacker. He didn't have an ounce of fat that I could see; he was cut everywhere. I looked away as he turned back to me.

"Can you stand up?" he asked.

I pushed up on my feet, wobbling a little, and tried to get my balance. "Yep."

"Can you walk?"

Of course I can't walk. I'm tied up. "No," I answered.

Suddenly he stepped right up to me. He put a hand on my back and one under my thighs, then squatted down and lifted me. My body stiffened. I was in this man's arms. He didn't have a shirt on. I had the curtain wrapped around my arms and waist, but I could feel his biceps and abs tighten up through the material. At least I knew that if he wanted drugs, he wasn't going to kill me in the next few minutes. But I was really wishing I could walk.

He carried me back across the hall into the bathroom and lowered me onto the vanity stool. I propped myself against the stool's scrolling metal back, using my feet to balance, and waited. Was I going to have to watch him take a shower? I really didn't want to see this man naked.

Holding onto the counter, he bent over, reached into his sneaker, and came up holding that small, black handgun. He set it on the counter alongside the other larger gun, my cigarettes, and the bottle of raspberry soda. Then, out of his pants he pulled a third handgun, also pretty small, and a small canister of pepper spray about the length of a cigarette lighter.

"Do you know what this is?" he asked, holding out the canister.

"Yeah," I said. "It looks like pepper spray or something." Why was he asking? Was he trying to scare me? I could just imagine him spraying it in my face as I sat here. I'd had a girl spray me with that stuff once—she was jealous that I was dating her ex-boyfriend—and it felt like a fire had exploded in my eyes.

Brian Nichols set the canister on the counter with that third gun; now I was looking at a row of black guns lined up all of two feet away from me. I didn't like the guns lying there, but at least they weren't being pointed at me. He must not have worried about leaving them out with me being tied up.

"Where do you keep the towels?" he asked, reaching into his pants pocket and pulling out a wad of bills. He set the money right there with the guns. *I wonder where he got that.*

Using my head to gesture toward the linen cabinet, I said, "Right there in that tall cabinet to the right of the door." *I really don't want to sit here and have to watch him do this. I don't want him getting any ideas about raping me.*

He opened the cabinet and pulled out a white bath towel, hand towel, and washcloth. Setting the stack on the counter near his red baseball hat, he grabbed the hand towel and turned toward me.

"I'm going to put this over your head so you don't have to watch."

"Okay," I said. *I can't believe this. Is this happening? Is he actually respecting me right now? Is he just modest?* I wondered if maybe he was beginning to see me for who I was—a real person with feelings and some dignity. *Could this actually be going my way here?*

He stretched out his arms and draped the hand towel over my head; in front it only hung down to about my nose. From underneath, I could see his legs from the knee down. I watched him step out of his black leather sneakers and kick them over toward the door, which he left standing open. Then he walked barefoot to the shower, and I heard him turn on the water.

As he undressed beside the tub, I saw his black suit pants drop to the floor and then a pair of white boxers. "Jail underwear," I thought.

I remembered going to visit Mack in the Richmond County jail when he was locked up for that DUI before I found out I was pregnant. As a visitor, I had to abide by certain rules. I couldn't wear anything too revealing. I could only bring Mack a limited amount of cash. And any articles of clothing—tee shirts, socks, and underwear—that I brought to him had to be white. Everything had to be white and sealed up in a brand-new package.

Sitting under the towel, I noticed that if I leaned forward slightly, I could see more of the bathroom and get a better look at what Brian Nichols was doing. Just to be sure he was going to get in the shower like he said, I leaned forward now, catching a glimpse of his rear as he was getting in. *Okay.* I backed up immediately. *Okay, I guess he's doing what he said he would do.*

Then I heard him step into the plastic tub and the curtain rings slide over the rod—and I knew Brian Nichols was in my shower.

8 do you believe in miracles?

As the bathroom steamed up, I decided I would start asking Brian Nichols some personal questions in my effort to get as close to him as I could. He didn't hurt me in that bedroom when he had the chance. He had just now respected me by covering my head with a towel. I found myself hoping, just a little, that things might get better for me, but I was also very aware the night could still go either way. I could just as easily die in this apartment as make it out of here alive; now, while I had a chance, I wanted to do whatever I could to shift the dynamic more in my favor.

"Do you have any kids?" I asked, raising my voice a little so he could hear me over the water. *I can't believe he didn't put that masking tape over my mouth.*

There was a pause. Then he answered in a low, flat tone. I strained to hear him. "I just had a son born."

What? Just had a son? And then he goes on a killing spree? Unbelievable. I wondered what it all meant—the birth of his son, then the shooting at the courthouse, then going on the run, all of it back to back. What was happening to this guy? He was totally unraveling here.

"Your son was *just* born?" I asked him. "Congratulations! That's amazing! You're a father. What's his name?"

I waited a few seconds, but he didn't answer. So I tried again.

He's got a child. I can use Mack in this right here. "You know," I said, "my husband was taken away—he died and didn't get to raise his little girl. Don't you want to raise your child?"

Another pause. "I'm never going to be able to raise him," he said, his voice muffled by the water. "I'm going to prison for the rest of my life."

I knew I had to turn that negative response around. I needed him to want to live—to see that there was hope if he would just stop running and hurting people. "If I could only get him to stop everything right here in this apartment," I began to think. "Just to stop and turn himself in." *This guy can't keep going like this, God. I don't want anyone else to die—not me, not even him.*

"Well, you never know what can happen," I said, lifting my voice and trying to sound upbeat. "You can still be involved in your son's life. Do you believe in miracles?"

No response. Just the sound of water hitting the tub. Then: "Yeah, I believe in miracles." *Thank you, God. Help me here.*

"Well, what do you think brought you here to my apartment? You know, you could've been killed out there, but you made it this far. You're in here taking a shower. You're alive—and you can still see your son. My husband doesn't have that chance. But you do."

From under the towel I watched the steam drifting out the bathroom door. He didn't answer. I listened to the water for a minute. I knew I needed to keep this going. I didn't want him to wonder what I was doing over here—to think I was trying to untie myself or get to those guns. I'm sure he knew there was no way I could get loose, but I didn't want anything to freak him out at this point. He said he wanted to relax. If I could just keep him calm, then maybe he would begin to trust me.

I tried another question.

"Where are your parents?" I wanted to stay focused on family to get his mind off of what he had been doing all day—killing people and running.

"They're in Africa," he said with little emotion. *Africa?* He didn't have an accent or anything. He just sounded tired, maybe depressed or irritated. *What does he think of me asking these personal questions right now—being bold and not acting scared?*

Before I had a chance to take the conversation any further, he turned off the water, and I heard him pull the shower curtain back. I could picture the tub—the cream-colored plastic running up the wall; the white rack for my shampoo and conditioner hanging on the showerhead; my washcloth from my shower this morning hanging on that rack; the plaid shower curtain. I had this fear that when I looked inside that tub again, I was going to see blood all in the bottom. Blood from the people Brian Nichols had killed.

Hearing the last of the water run through the drain, I could see from under the towel his dark feet step out of the tub, first onto my teal bath mat, and finally onto the orange rug closer to me. As he dried off, I could see the white bath towel flap below his knees. Then I could tell he was wrapping the towel around his waist.

I remembered the drugs—and that pink zipper pouch tucked under the fold of my comforter. Why did I even have it in the house? These days, since I was trying to straighten up, I always flushed the leftovers. I would get a little bit of ice every once in a while for a specific purpose—like staying up to study for a test or, in this case, staying up to move. Then, normally, I flushed whatever was left over down the toilet. I would tell myself, "See, I don't need this. I can stop when I want to. It's not ruling me. I can flush it, no big deal."

But for whatever reason, I had not flushed the leftovers from the move. I held onto the stuff. *Why did I do that?* Maybe I was thinking I didn't want to waste it. Maybe I thought I might need it again—I was trying to go to school at night and hold down two jobs. Still, this was the only time I had kept ice in my house in months. *And now, like a total idiot, I've offered it to this guy who's freakin' shot three people, broken into my apartment, and tied me up. Why didn't I keep my mouth shut? Why didn't I think before I spoke?*

"You got some clothes I can wear—like a tee shirt or something?" he asked. He had stepped to the door, and I could see by his feet that he was facing me where I sat with the towel still over my head.

"Yes," I said. At this point, what was mine was his. "I've got stuff that might fit you. Go in my bedroom. Boxers are in the bottom drawer of that short dresser by the windows."

I saw his feet turn, then a second or two later, I heard the drawer open. When I heard it close, I continued, raising my voice a little. "Okay, if you go over to the tall dresser, you can look in those larger drawers at the bottom and find tee shirts."

I was picturing my tee shirt drawers as I talked. They were color-coded. All of my clothes were organized by color and type. I couldn't help it—I was just a neat freak. If I wanted a white tank top, I would go to the tank top section of my closet and look for white. If it wasn't there, then I knew it was either dirty or someone had taken it and not put it back. My drawers were the same way—set up so I could find what I wanted when I wanted it.

Now, as I heard Brian Nichols opening my drawers in the tall dresser, I thought, "He's going to look in those drawers and think I'm a totally strange person." *But at least he'll see more about the kind of person I am, I guess.*

A minute later I could hear the sound of fabric stretching and sliding over skin—he was putting on a shirt. Then the drawer closed, and I saw his feet again. He stepped into the bathroom, reached out, and slowly pulled the towel from my head. I tried to shake and blow my blond curls out of my eyes so I could look at him.

He stood in front of me now, wearing the pair of blue boxers with white snowflakes that I had gotten out of the donations box when I was in my recovery program the year before. For three months I had slept in those boxers pretty much every night; and after working outside raking and bailing pine needles all day, I always slept hard. I liked the work, though—or, I grew to like it, both the work and the routine. At the beginning I hated everything about recovery. The program was out in the middle of nowhere several hours from Atlanta, and I could remember looking at my mom the day we pulled up to that house and thinking, "She can't be leaving me out here."

The tee shirt Brian Nichols had on—it was tight and pulling around his chest and shoulders—was my white Willie McGee's work shirt from waiting tables the summer before. I remembered my last day working there. I was being moved up from wait staff to bartender, and I was training behind the bar. As I practiced making drinks, I started feeling crazy and thinking people were after me. This was several months after recovery. I had gotten back in touch with my Augusta friends by then, and I was back into ice again. Standing behind the bar at Willie McGee's, I felt like I was losing my mind, and I could tell my coworkers were laughing at me. They could see what I was doing; they knew I was messed up. So I thought, "Well, if they're laughing at me and thinking I'm stupid, then what's the point of even coming to work?" After that, I didn't go in. And they fired me.

"Get up," Brian Nichols said.

I pushed myself up from the vanity stool, hopping in order to catch myself from falling.

"Can you walk now?"

What would make this guy think I can suddenly walk? "No," I said, "but I can hop." I definitely was not up for being carried again. I would rather hop around the rest of the night, falling down and busting my butt, than have him carry me.

"You hop in here and sit on the bed," he said, walking across the hall to the bedroom.

I followed him—hopping slowly in my sock feet so I didn't slip and trying to stay balanced despite having no real bend in my knees and my legs taped together—and I made my way to the edge of the bed where I had been sitting when he tied me up. His black blazer was still hanging on that post next to me.

As I turned my back to the bed and then leaned backward to sit down, I saw him coming toward me. *What's he doing?* He grabbed the knot of curtain material at my side and started working to untie it. *Am I being untied already? Is he actually feeling more comfortable with me? Or is this going to be bad, Lord?* I really hoped he wasn't going to ask me for those drugs.

He got the knot loose and unwrapped me, pulling the curtain away from my body and throwing it on the floor by my tall dresser. Then he bent over my legs and undid the knots in the extension cord. As he yanked at the cord, trying to loosen it and get it off my shins and knees, I could feel my legs relax a little and my circulation return. *Okay, get me ready for whatever's next.*

He got the cord off, stood up, and dropped it behind him near the curtain. Then he reached back and grabbed a pair of blue-handled scissors off my dresser. I hadn't seen those in here earlier—they came from the drawer by the stove in the kitchen. *What's he doing with those?*

Bending down to where the tape ended at my shins, he began cutting straight up the front of my legs, in between my knees and thighs until he had cut the tape all the way through. Then he peeled what now looked like a sheet of tape first off my right leg, thigh to shin; and then off the back of my legs, reaching his hands underneath to finally unwind all the tape off my left leg.

"Stand up," he said. I stood, bending my knees and straightening them a few times while he balled up the tape and dropped it on the floor. It felt good to be free of that stuff. "Now turn around."

I turned toward the bed and felt the cold metal of the scissors at the top of my wrists. He cut down between my hands to my fingertips and unwrapped the masking tape, picking off the stray pieces. *That feels better now. Lord, just help me keep it together.* I stretched my arms out to the sides and to the front, loosening up my shoulders. Then I turned back around and faced him.

"Okay," he said. "Now where's that stuff?"

9 defining moment

"Hold on," I said. "I'll get it."

I walked to the head of the bed on the left side—the side farthest from the windows and nearest the closet—and reached underneath where I had folded down the comforter, feeling for the pink zipper pouch. I kept the pouch under the fold, where it was easy to grab just in case the police ever busted in on me and I needed to get rid of the drugs fast. I probably came up with that hiding spot when I was messed up and paranoid and thinking the police were tracking me, but it worked for me.

"Hey," Brian Nichols said as I turned back around, "can I wash my clothes in here?"

Is he asking my permission? Okay. Maybe things are turning just a little in my favor. Please let it stay that way. I have no idea what's going to happen with these drugs.

"You can," I said. "But you're going to have to fix that washing machine first. It was spewing water everywhere earlier. But yeah. Go ahead."

Looking at him standing there in my boxers and tee shirt, I remembered some pants hanging in my closet. "And if you don't want to mess with the machine, I think I might have some pants in here that'll fit you. They're men's pants." I stepped over to the closet and walked into the bright light.

The closet was huge—it was one of my favorite things about this new place. Inside, my clothes were hanging along three walls, and underneath the clothes I had set up some stackable units from Wal-Mart for my shoes. In the corner just to my left was my set of plastic file drawers with a box of extra files sitting on top. Pants were hanging on the wall facing me.

All the way over on the right-hand side of the pants rack, I still had that pair of khakis belonging to a guy from Augusta who lived with me for a few months in my other apartment. He stayed with me around the time I was getting back into ice and working at Willie McGee's—late summer to early fall of last year. I was arguing with Aunt Kim on the phone a lot then. "This is not good enough," she would tell me. "You're living with that boy. We know you're doing drugs. You may have finished recovery, but you can't raise Paige like this." I just fought her and fought her, denying the drugs, and she kept on challenging me.

One day she called and said, "Ashley, I'm tired. I don't want to raise Paige. I want you to raise her. I want you to see her grow up. I want you to be here when she gets married. I want her to be able to look at you one day and say, 'Mommy, thank you for what you did for me. Thank you for teaching me.'" As Aunt Kim talked, her words started sinking into my heart, and I began to cry. "I want that too," I said. "I want that too."

Days later I got fired from Willie McGee's. My mom, who lived in Atlanta by then and could see what I was doing, told me it was a wake-up call. I thought, "She's right. This is it. I've got to make some changes." I told the guy living with me that he would have to move out.

Now I bent down and pulled that guy's pants off the hanger and walked back into the room.

"Here," I said, handing the khakis to Brian Nichols. "See how these fit."

He held them up for a second and folded them over his arm. Then I held out the pink zipper pouch. "Here you go."

He looked at the pouch. "How do you do it?" he asked. *Is he nervous? I hope so.* Then: "Aren't you going to do it with me?"

The words came out faster than I could think them. "No way," I said. "That stuff has ruined my life. Do it if you want to. But I'm not doing it."

Whoa! I couldn't believe what I had just said. *"I'm not doing it." Did I just say that?* I stopped for a minute to regroup. I had totally shocked myself. Holding that pouch out to Brian Nichols right then, I really and truly felt as if nothing he did or said could make me do that stuff with him. I wasn't even tempted to consider it. Not even the slightest bit. Snorting those drugs up my nose had absolutely no appeal to me. The whole thought of it actually repulsed me. *This is huge, Ashley. Totally huge.* I wondered if I had ever felt this turned off since first trying ice. I didn't think so. Not even during recovery.

Suddenly, looking down at my drug pouch, I realized that I would rather have died in my apartment than have done those drugs with Brian Nichols. Rather have died. Was I feeling this? Was this me? I felt as if I was seeing the truth like never before. Those drugs were my weakness. They were my baggage—the stuff I kept dragging around and trying to hold on to. I was trying to be what Paige needed with my two jobs and being in school so I could prove to my family that I was on my feet like those custody papers said. And I was reading my *Purpose-Driven Life* book; I was trying to show God I really was serious now. But then, I also wanted my drugs when I wanted them. Just a little bit here and there, I would tell myself; I can control it. And yet I couldn't totally let go. I was weak to those things. And it was dawning on me right here in my bedroom that God was really tired of me being weak.

Yes, I made it through recovery. But then I fell into that stuff again. Yes, I made some choices after that to snap out of it, clean up, and get back on the path. But I was still doing the drugs—so what if it was less often? I was doing them, and that was the bottom line here. There was that awful back and forth I would play with God about the guy who got the stuff for me. *Let him be there. Let him not be there.* I would repeat the whole line to myself: "But I'm in school now. I'm working two jobs. I'm getting it right. I'm making a home for Paige. Just this once or twice isn't going to hurt."

That was weakness right there. That was giving in. "But other Christians make mistakes. I bet other Christians have done drugs." No! God did not want me doing drugs, period. What other people did was their business—they would have to answer to God too. Right now all I could hear was God saying, "You know, Ashley, you've got to quit saying 'oops.' At some point you're going to have to start learning. Connect the dots. Look at what this stuff does to you and then ask yourself, 'Why am I still doing it?'"

Well, I was going to learn right now. Right this minute. I realized that even if God took me home tonight, this was it for those drugs. I was not doing that stuff anymore. I remembered what I had told Aunt Kim the day I took Paige over to her house and moved her in there for good: "I'm not stopping," I said, daring my aunt to challenge me. "You know, I would rather die than quit doing these drugs." Pulling out of her driveway, I told myself, "You are such a loser! You are sorry. You can't even stop for Paige? You won't let it go for your child?" I knew the answer, of course—it was no. To me, moving Paige in with Aunt Kim just gave me more license to get messed up as much as I possibly could.

But here I was, standing in front of Brian Nichols—a guy who was holding me hostage in my own apartment after a terrible killing spree—and thinking the complete opposite of what I had told Aunt Kim. I was actually thinking, "I would rather die because I *didn't* do those drugs than die doing them." If the cops were going to bust in here and find me dead, they were not going to find drugs in my body when they did the autopsy. I was not going to die tonight and stand before God, having done a bunch of ice up my nose. Jesus was not going to look at me and say, "Well, the last minutes of your life you did drugs." It just wasn't going to happen. I wanted God to be proud of me. I wanted to hear him say, "You made a good decision this time."

For once, when it counted, I was going to stand up for God and do what he wanted me to do. This right here—I knew this had to be the defining moment of my life. Until now, Mack's murder had been the defining moment. Everything had changed for me after that—changed for the worse. But right here in my bedroom, this seemed to me like the real defining moment; whatever happened after this, things were going to change in my heart for the better. Because even if I died tonight, I could still look at God and know that he was pleased with me for doing the right thing. He might not be pleased with me for offering those drugs, but that was just going to have to be Brian Nichols's choice at this point. As for me—finally, once and for all, I was going to do the right thing.

Brian Nichols stood there holding the pants and looking at the pouch. "Can you set it up for me?"

"Sure," I told him. "I'll set it up for you. But you know, I really wish you wouldn't do it. If you want to relax, this is definitely not the drug for you to be doing right now."

He didn't say anything, so I walked out of the room and took the pouch into the bathroom. *All right, it's his choice. He can do what he wants.* "Come on," I said.

Laying the pouch on the counter by the sink, I realized I didn't have a credit card.

"Hey," I called out to him. He was still in the bedroom. "I need my pocketbook."

"It's in the living room," he said.

I walked into the living room, and there it was—the fake Louis Vuitton from Aunt Kim—sitting on the coffee table over to my left. I couldn't believe he was just letting me walk around like this. The guns were lying out on the bathroom counter. What if I had grabbed one and walked back into the bedroom pointing it at him? I guessed my mind just hadn't gone there. For whatever reason, I was focused on doing what he asked: getting the drugs laid out for him so he could make his choice. I believed he was starting to feel comfortable with me, and I hoped that somehow everything going on in here right now might work to my advantage. I didn't know how I was going to get out of here, but I just kept my mind on trying to win his trust and do the next thing.

I reached into the pocketbook for my brown leather wallet and took out a supermarket card and a twenty-dollar bill. Then I dropped the wallet back into my bag and walked into the bathroom, standing to the left of the sink with one knee on the vanity stool.

Brian Nichols was still in the bedroom. On the long counter to my left were the three black handguns, the pepper spray, my cigarettes, the soda bottle, the wad of bills from his pants pocket, and his red baseball hat. The framed picture of Paige and me was just in front of where I stood beside the sink. I pulled the small tin—it was on a key ring—out of the pink zipper pouch and set it on the counter right in front of the photograph. I could just hear Paige's voice on the phone: "Mommy, when are you going to get better so I can come and live with you?" *God, I totally trust you. You do your will tonight. But you know she's expecting me to be there in the morning. You know how much she needs me.*

I opened the tin—the top read "You're a Loser, I'm a Goddess"—-and took out the little Ziploc bag with green 7's on it. In the bottom of the bag were the tiny crystals, like tiny pieces of glass—an amount about the size of my fingernail. I opened the bag and shook the ice out on the counter. I remembered being so good with this stuff, I could break it down and lay out a line on the armrest between the passenger and driver seats in my boyfriend John's car and then snort it up as he was driving. Either that or I'd hold the tray the ice was laid out on and snort it from there. I did that who knows how many times back and forth to Atlanta when we were making drug runs. I did it right after I got asked to leave my first recovery program for bad behavior. John came and picked me up at the place, and we went straight to Atlanta to the drug dealer's.

Now I opened up the twenty-dollar bill from my wallet and laid it flat on top of the ice. Then I picked up the supermarket card and started sweeping it back and forth over the bill to break the ice down into powdered form. As I worked, I heard Brian Nichols in the hall.

"I like your style," he said behind me suddenly. *You like my style?* I turned around and saw him looking into the living room. I guessed he meant he liked the style of my apartment, the way I had decorated it—my furniture or something.

"Thanks," I said, still holding the supermarket card.

Then he asked, "Have you ever dated a black guy?"

"No," I said. "I haven't." *He must be pretty relaxed now if he's asking me that.* I thought back to high school, how some of the black guys I played basketball with seemed to like my style. I was stylish in the way I dressed but pretty conservative, a typical preppy girl. I wasn't all into hip-hop like some of the white girls I knew who wore their pants hanging off their rears. I listened to rap a lot, but I was preppy and athletic. That was just me. Maybe those boys liked me for it. I didn't know.

Then, still facing the hallway, I noticed the way those khakis were fitting Brian Nichols. "Dude, you're wearing high waters!" I pointed down and started laughing. He looked ridiculous with those huge shoulders busting out of my tee shirt and the tight little khakis hitting him above the ankles. And now he was wearing a pair of my white socks too. I laughed really loud—just a free, bold laugh. *This feels great! It feels awesome to let this laugh out.* I felt myself relax for a minute for the first time in what felt like hours.

Brian Nichols didn't say anything, but I could see the corners of his lips turn up just a little as he looked down at his feet. "This is good," I thought. "I must be getting somewhere." Then he walked over to where I was breaking down the ice and stood in front of the sink at my right arm, watching me.

I lifted the twenty off the powder and set it to the side.

"That's all you got?" he asked, looking at the powder spread out flat on the white countertop. "Can you get any more?"

He doesn't know what he's getting into. "I promise you this is enough," I said. What I had lying there on that counter could last somebody who wasn't an addict at least twenty-four hours, maybe double that. Plus, what was he thinking—could I get him some more? Was he out of his mind? Did he think I was just going to leave him holed up in my apartment while I went out to make a drug run? *Sure! I can just hear it now. "Excuse me, I need some drugs for Brian Nichols. He's at my place waiting for it."*

I used the supermarket card to chop the ice up a little, and then I laid it out into one long line.

"Whoa," he said, raising his eyebrows. The amount looked bigger, now that it was laid out. Then he asked, "Now what?"

"Just do what you want of it," I told him, stepping back from the counter. "It's your choice. You can roll up that twenty sitting right there and snort it up if you really want to do it. But that's your choice, dude."

10 awakening

He looked over at the twenty-dollar bill, then back to the line. "You're really not going to do it with me?" he asked. He was still standing to my right at the sink.

I broke the one long line down into three smaller lines for him so he wouldn't try to do all of it at once. Then I leaned back against the long counter with the guns on it, and I looked him in the eye.

"Look," I said. "I don't think you understand. I told you that stuff right there has ruined my life. I'm a drug addict. Are you hearing what I'm saying? *A drug addict*. I'm weak to that stuff. If it's there, then I start thinking, 'Well, I might as well do it,' instead of finding a reason not to." I looked down at my feet for a minute, trying to control my emotions. For some reason I just wanted to start yelling, "Don't do it!" at this guy.

"You know," I said, shaking my head. "I can't even believe that stuff is sitting here in front of me right now. I'm not doing it. And I really wish you wouldn't, either. I wish I hadn't even offered it to you. It's just—it's just a really bad idea. Trust me on this."

He stood at the sink, looking into my face and listening.

"Actually," I said, "it's amazing I'm even standing here in front of you in this bathroom and not dead in some cemetery somewhere because of that stuff." Now I was looking him in the eye again. I wanted him to hear what I was saying. Those drugs were serious, and he needed to know.

I remembered coasting down that long hill on Hereford Farm Road after having met Aunt Kim at Paige's doctor appointment. That was two years ago now. It was just a week after I'd been released from the mental hospital, just days after I'd signed those custody papers for Aunt Kim. I had gone to Paige's doctor's appointment clean that day; I wanted to be in my right mind to see my daughter. And I had begged Aunt Kim, "Please let me take Paige with me for a little while—just let me take her to the park or somewhere and be with her. Please!" But Aunt Kim told me no, and she wasn't giving an inch.

"Okay," I thought, pulling out of the parking lot. "I've gotta do something here. I've just signed those custody papers. I've gotta get my child back. She won't even let Paige ride in the car with me. Something's not right about this. I have to take some action."

Right then it occurred to me that I should start looking for a job. That would help. At least, with a job I would be on the way to providing a "stable home" for Paige like the custody papers said. The idea seemed brilliant. That's exactly what I was going to do. Look for a job. "I'm clean," I thought. "I'll go right now."

I knew one of my tires was low on air, so I decided to stop first at a gas station on the top of a hill on Hereford Farm Road. I cranked up my music and drove on that smooth, winding road, thinking about where all I would go to put in job applications. Then, about a mile from the gas station I heard that voice in my head. It was so real. I was driving down a long hill. I wasn't even high. But I heard that voice—I was in a state of psychosis. Suddenly I started thinking I was hearing God tell certain people to come to heaven and others to stay on earth. Then I heard something say, "Let go and let God." I heard it so clearly. I thought it was God telling me to let go of the steering wheel.

"Okay, God," I said. "I'll test you. If you really are God, then I can let go and nothing's going to happen. You're going to drive this car for me. I'm supposedly your child, so let's see if you can do it." I was mocking God in a way, but in my heart I really wanted him to drive that car. I thought I would open my eyes and find my car stopped in the road down at the bottom of the hill.

Taking my hands off the wheel, I closed my eyes and put my head back. I remembered maybe the next half-second—the feel of the headrest and the way my arms felt in the air as I took them off the wheel. But I could never remember anything else. Nothing. I woke up two days later in the trauma unit at the hospital looking at my mom and my boyfriend John. They told me my car had crossed the median at a curve and gone off the road headlong into a ditch. I had been airlifted to the hospital. Both my arms were broken. I had three broken ribs and a severed pancreas. I could've been dead.

"That stuff makes me crazy," I told Brian Nichols now, pointing at the lines on the counter. "My nickname used to be 'Crazy Girl.' Literally, there were times I thought I was losing my mind because of those drugs and doing permanent damage to my brain. Once my mom and my aunt had to put me in the mental hospital—that's how bad it got. I thought I was having a complete breakdown. I hear voices when I'm on ice. I think people are after me. I get scared. Scared of what? I don't know. Scared of anything."

Fear. I had written that down during one of my morning devotions not long ago. I was answering a question in my *Purpose-Driven Life* book about what drove my life—or what my family and friends would say drove my life. *Fear,* I put down. *Fear and drugs.*

"The reason I don't have my little girl right now is because of those drugs," I said, pointing at the photograph of Paige and me on the counter right behind the lines. "I can't even provide a stable home for her. Can't even raise her. My family doesn't trust me. And why should they? I've lied to them so many times." Now I felt disgusted with myself.

"I'm not doing that stuff anymore. I mean, it's over! Those drugs make me miserable. It's just a total state of misery. I think I'm going to have all this energy to get things done, but then I just get confused and paranoid and miserable. I stay up all night and I can't think. I keep asking myself, 'Why, Ashley? Why are you doing this to yourself? Your child deserves better. You're destroying your life, and she needs you.' But then I just keep doing it. And I stay scared. Really scared."

I thought back to February—just last month—sitting in Aunt Kim's church with that dollar bill I'd used to snort drugs, getting ready to drop it in the offering basket for my *Purpose-Driven Life* book. Something had to change for me right then, and I knew it. I felt like God was pounding on my door. I was terrified. The fear was just huge. I kept asking myself, "What's going to happen to me?" I could hear Satan whispering, "It's okay. You can do those drugs. Now and then won't hurt." But God was saying, "No! It's not okay. It's never okay. I'm right here. You can stop." And yet I wasn't stopping. I could go weeks without it. I could flush the stuff down the toilet. *See, I can stop.* But I couldn't stop. "Just this once," I kept hearing. "It won't hurt anything."

I put my left hand on the counter by the sink and leaned on it, glancing down at that photograph of Paige and me. Brian Nichols had not moved. He was standing in front of the sink, and his eyes were fixed on my face. So I started again.

"This right here—this whole thing with you being here in my apartment right now and wanting this stuff—this is God's way of telling me, 'Look, Ashley, stop now. I'm giving you one more chance. You better stop right now, little girl, or I'm bringing you home. You are my child, and if you can't stop right now—right here when you're in this kind of situation—then you're never going to stop. And then what would be your point on earth? I'm giving you this challenge. If you can do this, then you can stay here and do my work here on earth. Or you can choose this other way of living, being miserable, and I'll just go on and bring you home with me. It's your choice.'"

I noticed that I had stepped away from the counter and was using my hands as I talked. Brian Nichols had his arms crossed over his chest now. The sleeves of my tee shirt were pulling around his biceps. "What's he thinking," I wondered. "Have I blown this guy away?" *I hope it's making him think, and think hard, about the choice he's about to make.*

Looking at him right then, I suddenly realized I didn't feel afraid anymore. I wasn't afraid of him. I wasn't afraid of what might happen to me in this apartment. I truly felt peaceful—as if God was just next to me. I couldn't believe it. There was no fear. *I'm not scared right here. I'm okay.* I had already made my decision—I knew I wasn't touching those drugs—and right now that seemed like all that mattered. That was what God wanted. I was doing what he wanted, and he was right here with me. *It's okay. I'm right here. You can stop.* God was helping me. I was stopping like he said. And I wasn't afraid.

Just then a phrase popped into my head from the twelfth step in my AA book: *"Having had a spiritual awakening as the result of these steps."* A spiritual awakening. I could remember Miss Kate, our instructor in recovery, talking about the spiritual awakening in our meetings. She always told us that our spiritual awakening might not be some huge, incredible moment. Most people, she said, came to a gradual understanding of who they were as addicts and how they needed to live. But I had read some really powerful stories in my AA book about people's eyes being opened, and I always wanted the big moment. I wanted something amazing to happen for me that would open my eyes and change me for good.

Standing in my bathroom now, with Brian Nichols and those lines of ice on the counter, I realized I was having my spiritual awakening right here in this apartment. Tonight—this was it. The spiritual awakening. Right here, as a hostage, my eyes were finally being opened: I was a drug addict, just like I had told Brian Nichols. I really was a drug addict.

Maybe I wasn't ever truly convinced of that before, even when I was at recovery. Leaving the program, I didn't want to do drugs anymore, but I didn't completely close the door, either. I thought maybe I would be able to use ice again. Maybe once in a while. Maybe on the weekends. And I tried that. But tonight I was seeing the stark reality of who I was. Drugs and I could never mix. I would never be able to do them, not on the weekends or any other time. I had to close the door—close it for good. And I was doing it. God was helping me. I had already decided. I was standing in my apartment with my life on the line, having my spiritual awakening, and saying, "No. I'm done. It's over."

I watched Brian Nichols for a few seconds. *What's he going to do?* He cleared his throat but didn't say anything. *Is he still going to do it? After everything I've said?* Then I saw him look at the three short lines on the counter. *Lord, let your will be done.*

"You know," I said again, pointing at that counter, "I really wish you would just leave that alone. It's gonna ruin your life. The first time I tried that stuff I was hooked—just gone. If I were you, I wouldn't go near it. It's not worth it. It'll be a huge mistake." *Forgive me for offering it to him.*

But Brian Nichols didn't answer me. He was still looking at the lines.

"Okay," I said. "It's your choice. Do what you want. But I'm not staying around for it. I don't want you to do it. I don't think you should do it. But I can't stop you."

Tucking my hair behind my ears, I turned and walked out into the hallway.

11 spiritual warfare

I leaned in the hallway doorframe facing the living room and could hear him moving things around on the bathroom counters. I heard him fumble with something. *Is he rolling up that twenty?* Then I heard his deep inhale. He had snorted a line up his nose. *He really did it. I just hope it doesn't make him crazy. Thank you that it isn't me in there.*

I could almost feel what Brian Nichols would have felt right then—the awful burning in his nostril and sinuses, the tears coming out of his eyes. It was really, really painful snorting that stuff. It was just miserable.

I turned back toward the bathroom now and looked over at him. He was standing up by the counter, facing the tub and looking down. I tried to read his face. He didn't look like he had even flinched. His eyes weren't running. His face was still. He wasn't gasping. Usually that burning lasted for a while. *Well, man, it sure hurts me to snort those drugs—not him, I guess.* When he looked over at me, I saw a little trace of white powder on the rim of his nostril.

Without saying anything, Brian Nichols walked past me out of the bathroom and turned into the living room. I glanced over at the guns lying on the counter and went to sit down on the vanity stool. *I just hate guns—hate those things lying there right now.* Two lines were still laid out near the picture of Paige and me; the rolled-up twenty lay off to the side near my pink zipper pouch and the tin. I looked at the lines and thought to myself, "When I was free to do whatever I wanted, I was a total prisoner to that stuff. Now I'm a hostage and I'm freer than I've ever been in my whole life. I'm really, really done."

Then I thought: "Okay—I'm stuck in this apartment with this guy. So I guess I can really be myself now. I can let out that person inside of me, the one I've been afraid to be. Right here I can live proclaiming the name of Jesus. Who cares if God isn't popular or whatever? So what if people would call me a holy roller? They're not here right now. It's just me and this guy and you, God. We're in here. And I'm done with those drugs. All of that is over. I'm living for you."

I heard Brian Nichols walking in the living room and then the kitchen. I stood up quickly right then and stepped toward the shower. The curtain was partially open, so I leaned forward and looked into the tub. *No blood in there. Good. Thank you. I just didn't want there to be blood in my bathtub.* I sat right back down and waited. I didn't see his sneakers or dirty clothes on the floor anymore, so he obviously moved those somewhere else. I wondered what time it was—I just had no idea. Maybe an hour or two had gone by. Maybe less. I couldn't gauge.

Brian Nichols walked back into the bathroom now, carrying a twelve-ounce can of Coors Light and another pack of cigarettes—Marlboro Lights. He must have gone out to the truck and gotten those.

"Want a beer?" he asked, holding his up. Then he stepped to my left, reached his arm over the counter, and lit that burgundy candle next to the picture of Paige and me using his pink lighter.

"No, thanks," I said. I didn't want beer—I sure wasn't going to sit back and party with him. All I wanted was God right now. I wanted to make God smile, like it said in my *Purpose-Driven Life* book. That's what I wanted.

Brian Nichols walked over to the toilet and sat down on top of the lid. I figured he was still more comfortable staying at the back of the apartment in a room with no windows, but at this point I began to think the police really weren't coming. I was amazed, totally amazed, that none of my neighbors had heard me scream. Or maybe someone heard me but then thought it was nothing. I didn't get it. I was screaming my lungs out. *Oh well, God, I trust you. This is your thing in here.*

Leaning back on the toilet, Brian Nichols was only a few feet away from where I sat on the vanity stool in front of the sink. The toilet was to the right of the sink, and all the way to the right, against the wall, was the bathtub. He stared straight ahead and took swigs of his beer. He really did look pretty relaxed. "He's just done that ice," I thought, "which is going to speed him up. And now he's drinking beer to slow down a little." *As long as he stays mellow like this. Just let him stay calm and not start acting crazy.*

Back when I was getting messed up on ice twenty-four-seven, I used to try and slow myself down. Not with beer, though. With Xanax. Mack and I had discovered Xanax about two months before he died. He smoked pot every day, and once he found Xanax, he started taking that pretty much daily too. Mack was angry. He was moody. He was always looking for something to take the edge off. And I was going to do whatever he did. That was just the kind of wife I was.

On Friday nights Mack and I would rent a limo with a bunch of friends and go out drinking and doing drugs—lots of times taking both ecstasy and Xanax. The combination made me feel free to do whatever I wanted, as if I didn't have a care in the world. Mack was a lot of people's hook-up for ecstasy. A guy we knew went to Atlanta to get it and then distributed the pills to a few people to sell; Mack was one of them—so we were pretty popular. The first time I met Mack we were at a party at a friend's house, rolling on ecstasy.

After Mack died and I dove hard into ice, I would do Xanax with that too. I would crank my body way up on ice, then slam it into reverse with Xanax. I did it all the time. I sped up. I slowed down. Up and down. It was amazing I lived through all that. I could already count three people I knew who had died that way—mixing up drugs.

Sitting on the vanity stool now, I felt a wave of gratitude to God come over me. For a second I couldn't believe I was sitting here—that I had actually made it this far. I mean, I wasn't dead. I was here in this apartment and in my right mind. I wasn't crazy from those drugs and off in some loony bin somewhere with permanent brain damage. For some reason I was still here. It was amazing to me right then. Aunt Kim always said I had nine lives. Now if I could just make it out of this apartment. If I could just have another chance to do things right. *If you're willing, God, you can bring me out of this. You can get me out of here so I can raise Paige and live for you. I'm ready to do it. I want to do it!*

—

Brian Nichols turned to face me, leaning forward over his knees with his beer in his hand. He started asking me questions, and our talk snapped back and forth to different subjects.

"What do you think about outer space?" he asked.

What? Outer space? I don't know, buddy. Maybe you're from there. "I don't know," I said, raising my eyebrows at him.

—

"What do you think about the war going on in Iraq?" He looked me in the eye and waited.

At least I could kind of answer this one. "The guys who go over there and protect us and die for our country—they're really brave. And we should be a lot more grateful to them."

—

"Did you play any sports in high school or anything?"

"Yeah," I said, stretching my legs out in front of me. "I played basketball in high school. I started on varsity in ninth grade and went to Duke University basketball camps and all that. I did the whole nine. I was going for a college scholarship, but then I got burned out on it."

I thought back to what my grandpa used to say after I graduated from high school and started running with those drug dealers and shoplifting: "You've thrown it all away! We've pulled for you and spent thousands of dollars on you and given you everything to succeed and you've thrown it all away!"

I could remember sitting in my car before my games my senior year and rolling joints in my lap so I could smoke pot on the way to the Lakeside High School gym. Either that, or I would go to this one friend's house and sit on the back porch smoking; then I would drive over to the gym and dress out. My justification was that I scored more points when I was high—I was relaxed and giddy and just played better, I thought. But then again, my attitude was really poor. College scouts would come, and I would just freak out on the refs who called fouls on me. The scouts probably thought, "Well, what happened to her? She wasn't like this last year."

"Yeah," Brian Nichols said, sipping his beer. "I played football in college."

That made sense—that he had gone to college. I knew by the way he was talking that he wasn't some hard criminal off the street. He spoke well. Even in asking me about the Iraq war, he seemed concerned about what was going on in the world. He seemed like he *knew* what was going on in the world—definitely more than I did.

"Are you a born-again Christian?" he asked. He had set his beer on the floor and now was smoking one of his cigarettes.

"Yes, I am." I was leaning forward on the stool with my elbows on my knees. "I asked Jesus into my heart when I was seven." This was good that he had asked me about God. I knew this was good. He had a church background, so I was going to connect with him on it right here.

"I was in church with my grandparents," I said. "My mom—she was a single mom until I was almost twelve; and I spent a lot of time with my grandparents when I was growing up. They lived right across the street for a while in the same apartment complex, and I would just go on over there after school or in the evenings or whenever my mom wanted to go do something or was working late. 'Go walk across the street to Mema's,' she would say. 'Be a good girl.' I was the only grandchild who didn't have a daddy around.

"So I went to church with Mema and Papa every Sunday—it was this little church in a pretty bad part of town. My grandpa was a preacher. He preached all over Augusta—that's where I lived. He was the headmaster at the Christian school where I went for a long time too. Anyway, this one Sunday, I was sitting there with Mema and Papa listening to some preacher, and he was talking all about hell and everything, and it just scared me to death. So I went up to Papa afterward and said, 'I don't want to go to that fire place. I want Jesus in my heart.' And he took me into a back room and prayed with me to receive Jesus in my life.

"But I got away from God for a long time," I said. I leaned over and reached across the counter for my cigarettes; they were near the guns. Brian Nichols handed me the pink lighter. The ashtray was between us next to the sink, on the edge of the counter closest to him.

"I mean," I continued, lighting my cigarette and taking a long drag, "I tried to do the God thing in high school—that's when I left Christian school and started going to public school. I still did my Bible study every night and went to youth group at this big Baptist church where I went with my mom and step-dad and my aunt and my cousins. But then I got away from all that, you know, and just started doing my own thing—I did things *my* way." I stopped for a second to smoke and ash my cigarette. "I mean, I got into drugs and everything."

I was thinking about my daddy now and some of his struggles. I was wondering how much of the whole drug thing was genetic. I remembered back when I would freak out on ice, and Paige would be around, and I would get so scared: "God, what if this really is hereditary and it's already in her bloodline? And now she's seeing her mama do it and it's just going to be this terrible cycle I'm dragging her into."

What made me fall into it so hard? Really, I just liked the drugs—how they made me feel. I tried pot for the first time at a party when I was drunk, and I threw up everywhere. But a week later I was at it again. And soon I got my first bag and practiced rolling joints and then started smoking all the time. I was totally relaxed on the stuff and loved it. I skipped my last class at school for fifty-two days my senior year to go sit with this guy I knew and smoke pot in his room with the window open. And suddenly I had all these new friends—the cool people. Before that, I was so locked into basketball and my family I didn't really have any close friends.

And I didn't think my family wanted to see the loneliness. We were a totally close-knit family—my grandparents, my mom, Aunt Kim, Uncle David, and all the spouses and kids. Everybody came to my basketball games and stood on the sidelines screaming for me. I knew they loved me. But this loneliness in me—they didn't seem to see it. Or the exhaustion of all that discipline: Basketball. Exercise. Cleaning the house. Cooking dinner and helping with my little brother and sister. I just burned out. I was tired of being what I thought everybody wanted. Tired of trying to be perfect. And now I had some cool friends to do stuff with, and we were having fun—or what I thought was fun. But then it just got bad—with cocaine and drug-dealer friends and getting in trouble and, later, failing out of Augusta College after that first semester. Just bad.

"So I got away from God," I said to Brian Nichols. "But now I want him more than ever. I want him to be proud of me. I want to get my life right—you know, get it on track. I've got to get it on track for my little girl."

"Are *you* a born-again Christian?" I asked him now, propping my elbow on the counter. I wanted to know. I assumed he would say yes, but I wanted to ask. He had asked me, so now it was my turn.

"Yeah." He put out his cigarette, then picked up his beer and took a swig. He didn't say anything else.

"Well," I said, "that means you're my brother in Christ, and I'm your sister in Christ."

I was trying to get him to identify with me on this. Whatever he would let me in on about himself, I was going to find the points we had in common and emphasize those—make those points huge. *See, we're just alike*. That's what I wanted him to keep hearing in his mind.

Then he said: "I think there's a demon inside of me—but I'm a child of God." *Whoa! What? What does he mean? That's freakin' nuts. How could the words* demon *and* child of God *be in the same sentence? How could a child of God have a demon in him?*

I was confused, but I could see he was wrestling with himself. He kept shifting—leaning back, then sitting forward. I said, "You need to ask God for forgiveness for what you've done, and he'll forgive you. That's what the Bible says."

I could see anxiety coming up in him. His brow was lowered. His head was bent toward the ground. *He's fighting. He knows what he did was wrong, but he knows the Word of God says he can be forgiven. He's just got to believe that. He's got to believe in forgiveness right now.*

"I've got this demon in me," he said again. "Just—I need to get it out of me."

I thought back to the way his eyes looked when he first came into the house—when he took off that baseball hat and told me who he was: "*Now* do you know?" he had said, opening his eyes wide and staring at me with that awful expression on his face.

I had looked into his eyes then, and I could see something really bad was happening inside of him. He did look as if he could have a demon in him. But now, sitting on top of the toilet in my tee shirt and those short pants after his shower, he looked different. His eyes looked different. He looked sad and afraid—but human. And this was *after* doing the drugs, which seemed strange to me. Those drugs always made me look crazy, especially in the eyes—just revved up and out of my mind. But not him. He looked more human now than he had all night.

"It's spiritual warfare," he went on. *Okay. I know that term. Aunt Kim uses it.* "I feel like God and Satan are fighting—fighting to take me. One or the other." He was looking at the wall straight ahead of him, squinting, and his face was really tense.

God and Satan fighting. That was serious. That was no joke. I understood that—all the back and forth. Just like what happened with me over those drugs: Satan saying, "Just this once won't hurt." And then God saying, "You can stop. I'm here."

I thought, "God and Satan are fighting in this apartment right now. Right here in my bathroom. They're fighting over this guy. God's trying to tug him one way; Satan's trying to tug him the other way. Which way will he go? What will he choose? He's just got to stop running. He's got to stop running and turn himself in."

13 pressing

"My people—people of my color—they needed me," he said now. He was rubbing his eyes with his hands, sitting forward over his knees. "They needed me for a job, and I had to be a soldier for my people."

I didn't say anything for a few seconds. I just smoked and looked at him. I thought about what he had just said. He was talking about being a soldier when he first came into my apartment, and I thought he was flipping out. Now, I thought, maybe I could address what he was saying here and try to relate with him about it and make some kind of connection. If people of his color needed him, then somewhere he was dealing with prejudice. How could I assure this guy that I wasn't looking at him and feeling prejudice toward him? I had to get him to trust me.

Something popped into my head right then—something I had seen at the mall when I was on my way to work at Express just the other day. *I can't tell him that.* I felt really bad about what had gone through my head at the time. I felt ashamed—and I thought it might make him mad. *Should I tell him this story? I want to tell him. I want to try and get him to see who I am.*

"Let me tell you this story about what I saw the other day," I said. "And—I want you—just, please don't get mad at me. Because I thought something really hateful about this black guy I saw, but I want to try and explain what I really felt so you can know more about who I am."

I reached over and ashed my cigarette in the ashtray between us on the counter. He didn't say anything. He just watched me.

"So I was on my way to work, and I saw this young black guy walk out of the mall, and he was holding a cup in his hand. He was holding a cup, and he took a sip of whatever it was, and then he just threw the cup down in the parking lot and walked off. Well, I got pretty ticked about that, and I thought this really bad, just evil thing about him. I wish I hadn't thought it, but I did.

"Then, not three seconds later, another black man, maybe in his late thirties or early forties, walks out of the mall, sees the same cup, goes and picks it up, and puts it in the trash. And I thought, 'Okay. Now there's a real man.'

"I don't know why I thought what I did about the first guy. Maybe I was harder on him because he was black, but I honestly didn't think I was. The point is, he was just acting like he could trash the world and let somebody else pick it up. And that's exactly what happened—somebody else came and was responsible and picked it up. It wasn't a color thing to me. I was looking at those two guys and thinking about their actions—I was trying to make my judgment on what they did."

I stopped talking and glanced over at Brian Nichols. What did he think? I couldn't tell. He looked past my head and said nothing. He shifted where he was sitting on top of the toilet and leaned back. I wanted him to know I wasn't looking at his color and judging him by that. I mean, I wasn't perfect. I did think that evil thought about that guy. But I hoped Brian Nichols saw what I meant. *I was trying to make my judgment on what they did.*

"I've got a plan," he said. He was leaning forward again now, with his elbows on his knees and his fingers laced together. The khakis were pulling around his thighs and riding really high up his shins. His beer can sat on the floor in front of him. "I've got this plan—it's to rob a bank."

No. He's got to stop. He can't do that. He's got to turn himself in.

"I'm going to rob a bank," he went on, "and I need your help."

Well, that's never going to happen. I'm not getting in trouble like that. I know what jail's like, and there's no way.

"Whoa, dude!" I said. "I'm not helping you rob any bank." Was this why he asked me earlier if I'd ever shot a gun? So I could help pull off a bank robbery?

I thought for a minute about the guns sitting behind me on the counter. What if he picked one of those up and threatened to blow my head off if I didn't agree to help him? It could happen. And if it did, I thought, I would just have to deal with it. Really, if I helped him rob a bank, I might as well let him go ahead and kill me right here because I would just get killed in the robbery anyway. And then what would that look like? Killed robbing a bank with someone I didn't even know. Not happening.

"But you'd be set for life," he said, looking me in the eye. "You'd be set."

Is he crazy? What makes him think he'd ever make it out alive to live off the money? "Look," I said, taking a deep breath, "I'm just not helping you do that, okay?"

He turned his head away and stared down at the beer can. To me, he looked even more exhausted than when he first came into my apartment. His skin looked like it was sagging under his eyes. I could see the lines in his forehead. He seemed depressed—just really down. Had my response brought him down even more? I mean, I wasn't robbing a bank with him. And he must've seen I wasn't going to move on that.

I was working on another cigarette now and looking at that picture of Paige and me up on the counter. Suddenly I felt my face flush and tears come up.

This guy wants to rob a bank. He's still thinking about running. I'm really not going to make it out of here, am I? I'm going to die and I'm never, ever going to see Paige again. What is she going to feel like? She's not going to have a mom or a dad. She's just going to be sad forever.

I knew my little girl. Even being away from her, I knew her heart. Whenever I saw her, she just ran up to me and jumped into my arms yelling, "Mommy! Mommy!" She grasped on to me and wouldn't let me go. It was as if there was a hole in her heart because I had been gone for so long—for two years she had been with Aunt Kim, and even before that, when she lived with me, I had checked out on her emotionally. I tried to see her as many weekends as I could now, but it didn't always work out between school and my jobs. And she just hurt over it. I knew she did.

I reached across the counter now, over the two lines of ice, and picked up the picture in its gold frame. Then I turned it toward Brian Nichols so he could see it. "This is Paige, my five-year-old little girl," I said. "She doesn't have a daddy."

I put my cigarette out in the ashtray and pulled the picture back, looking at Paige in that beautiful white dress and running my hand over the glass.

"I'm supposed to see her in the morning at ten o'clock," I said. "Am I going to be able to do that?" I kept my eyes on Paige as I talked—the white dress, her little pug nose. I needed to leave at 9:30 if I was going to get there on time.

"No," he said.

Then the tears came, and I couldn't hold them in. "I haven't seen her in two weeks," I said, sobbing freely now and looking him in the face, "and she's expecting me to be there. She doesn't have a father, and for her not to have her mommy there too—she's going to be devastated."

He sat there watching me. Then he said, "Well, maybe I'll let you call them."

I shook my head and laid the picture frame in my lap. "You don't understand. My family's going to be worried if I just call them and don't show up. That's not going to be enough—for me to just call. They'll be worried. And Paige will be really upset without me there. She hasn't seen me in so long."

I had to keep pressing. For years I had tried to put myself in Paige's shoes, to feel her feelings about not having a daddy. I knew what it was like not having my daddy around growing up—it hurt me. I was afraid of my daddy. Every time he called, which wasn't much, he slurred his words; and I was scared even to come to the phone when my mom told me he was asking for me.

But at least my daddy was alive. At least I could believe that maybe one day things would get better. Paige just had this end—her daddy was never coming back. She couldn't even have hope. And now for me to not be there tomorrow? I wanted Brian Nichols to feel that. I wanted him to put himself in her position—to think about Paige first not having a daddy and then really expecting to see her mommy after not having seen her for two weeks. I just had to make him feel that.

I was looking right at him with tears running out of my eyes. "I can't not be there," I said, talking low, barely able to get the words out. "I can't not show up. She's five years old. Imagine how long two weeks is when you're that little. I can't do that to her."

Then I said, "And I'm supposed to work tomorrow too. And they're going to wonder why I'm not there if I don't come in." *I'm really reaching here, God. Help me out. Help me!*

He was quiet for a second, looking down at the linoleum floor. "Maybe," he said, now raising his head. "Maybe I'll let you go. Just—I don't know. Let's just see how things go."

"Okay," I answered, wiping my cheeks with my hands. *God, thank you. Thank you for a foot in the door. Just keep helping me. I've got to make more progress. Please.*

13 the one who paid

So what happened to your husband?"

He lit a cigarette and sat up straight on the edge of the toilet seat. His voice was still flat and low. He seemed melancholy to me. Not at all like I was when I did those drugs, with my brain going a hundred miles an hour just zinging all over the place. Maybe God was overriding the drugs and really calming him down to show me, "Look, even though this is bad and I don't want you doing this, I'm going to use it to your advantage right now." I hoped so. I really hoped so.

"Well," I said, "my husband Mack died on a Friday night when we were out." I thought I would really start sharing with Brian Nichols now. I wanted to open up my life to him so he could learn more about who I was and feel what I felt. I thought maybe if he could get to know me and understand my life a little, he would want to let me go see Paige in the morning. So I started.

"You know, what happened to Mack that night—it just wasn't supposed to end that way. All week leading up to the night he died, I was having these anxiety attacks. And I'd never had those before. I mean, I just felt shaky, not in control—like something bad was going to happen. I would tell Mack, and he'd just say, 'Well, honey, you look horrible—go lie down.' But I still had them.

"And that night when we were getting ready to go out, I didn't feel good, either. But Mack wanted to go out, so we did. Because that's just how I was—I was going to do whatever he did. And we actually got home early. But then Mack heard that this guy he knew had called him a narc, so he wanted to go slap him around some. I just fought it and fought it. I didn't want him to go out again, but he was going, so I went with him. And we never made it back. He died there in the apartment complex after that fight. He was just gone. They wouldn't even let me identify his body."

I could see that parking lot again—the lights spinning on the police cars, the paramedics and that machine, and Mack lying there not responding. And I remembered the sense of evil I felt standing there when the police wouldn't let me get in the ambulance and identify Mack's body. "But I'm his wife!" I shouted. "We're sorry, ma'am," they said. And that was it. Daniel McFarland Smith Jr. was gone. They took him away. I could feel evil all around me. And a horrible sense of darkness. Like nothing that had happened there was of God.

—

"I felt so alone after that," I told Brian Nichols, pulling my cigarettes off the counter and taking another one out. "Just so alone. I was never mad at God. I asked him why, but I wasn't mad at him. I was just numb, I think. I made myself numb. Instead of being a real woman about the situation and facing my feelings, I took drugs so I didn't have to feel. I took pain pills for an entire year—tons of them. And then I would get them from pharmacies and sell them to people. That made me popular, I guess. My phone was ringing all the time, and I didn't feel so alone.

"And then later I got into that other stuff—I got weak and tried ice and went completely off the deep end. And you know what? Paige is the one who paid. She lost her daddy, and then her mommy was selfish and started destroying herself. And she's the one who paid."

I had laid the gold picture frame down on the counter, and now I picked it up and looked at Paige again. Tears just started coming. "I mean, imagine how she feels," I said, holding up the frame to him again, tears running down my face now. "She doesn't have a daddy—didn't even get to say goodbye to him. And now I'm not around, either. I'm miles and miles away, not even fit to be her mother right now."

I set the frame down and lit my cigarette. It felt good to smoke, good to inhale, good to really cry. Brian Nichols was just sitting there on top of the toilet, listening, watching me.

"After Mack," I said, wiping my face, "I felt like I would never be able to take care of Paige and provide for her. I was scared to do it by myself. Didn't think I could do it without a man—without my husband. And, well, my husband wasn't around. And if I wasn't going to be able to succeed, or even survive really, then why try? So I basically gave up right there at the beginning. Once we had the funeral, it was just a constant party at my house. Literally, right after the funeral people were over smoking pot, drinking, and taking pills; and someone said, 'This is the way Mack would want it.' And I was like, 'No—it's not the way he would want it.' But I didn't stop it. The party went on, and people kept bringing me drugs.

"Sometimes we smoked pot in front of Paige. I took pills in front of her. 'Mommy's just taking medicine' is how I looked at it. Once I started ice, I never did *that* in front of her—I mean, people smoked it in the next room, but I didn't actually do it where she could see me. But I would take care of her when I was messed up on it—messed up and really paranoid that people were after me. And I drove her around in the car like that."

I thought back to that hill on Hereford Farm Road and how I had begged Aunt Kim at Paige's doctor's appointment: "Please, just let me take her for a couple of hours—just to the park or something. I want to be with her. Please! Can't I take her?" But Aunt Kim said no. She said no. And I thanked God for that—for saving Paige's life. Because that was what happened when Aunt Kim said no. I remembered that voice in my head again as I was driving. *Let go and let God.* I just knew it was God talking to me. I just knew he wanted me to let go of that steering wheel. "I'm going to test you," I had said. And then there was the way my hands felt in the air and my head going back. And then nothing.

I paused and smoked for a few seconds, remembering what it was like waking up in the hospital trauma unit. "Baby, what happened in that car?" John had asked me. "What happened to you?"

"And so," I told Brian Nichols, "I gave Paige to my aunt. I gave my aunt temporary custody of her. I got released from the mental hospital and a couple days later went to sign some papers at the lawyer's office. Really, I just had to do it. I loved Paige so much, and I knew I wasn't going to stop using the drugs. She couldn't be with me in all of that. I was starting to feel like something bad was about to happen, and I knew she couldn't be around for it. I thought she'd be better off with my aunt until I could get my life together. Actually, that's what I'm doing in Atlanta right now. Trying to get my life together for Paige."

He sat quietly, listening, not really shifting around much. He wasn't smoking or sipping his beer anymore. Just listening.

I looked over at the three black guns. They just made me nervous sitting there. I mean, what if one went off? I had a friend whose gun had gone off and blown a hole right through his car. The gun just fired. I could picture that happening here. *Girl dies in hostage crisis from a gun accident.* Nuts! The thought just creeped me out. I looked up at my linen cabinet by the door. I knew the top shelf had nothing on it. Maybe I could get him to agree to put those guns up there. He was listening to me. I knew he was hearing my story and paying attention. Maybe he would trust me enough to feel that he could do it. He seemed calm. *Oh well, can't hurt to ask.*

"Look," I said to him, putting out my cigarette and reaching my hand back to point at the guns. "Don't you want to put those things up? Just—what if one goes off? There's a cabinet right there." I looked over at the linen cabinet. "Top shelf's empty." *Is this a totally stupid move, or what?*

I turned back to him to see what he would do. His eyes kind of glazed over. He sat up a little straighter. Then he looked me in the eye and shook his head. "No," he said. And that was all. *Man, I'm an idiot. I should never have asked. Did I just undo everything I was working for? Stupid!*

"I'm here in Atlanta," I said now, "because I needed a fresh start—I had to get away from my past in Augusta and the old crowd and all the drugs and everything." I wanted to get this conversation back on track. I had to keep pushing—bringing him into my life. And just make him feel like a normal person who I was sharing my life story with. *See, I'm trusting you with my whole life. Don't you think you can trust me too?* That's what I wanted him to see.

"My Aunt Kim is still in Augusta, which is why Paige doesn't live near me. Pretty much my whole family lived in Augusta until last year. Now it's just my grandparents and Aunt Kim's family. My Uncle David and his family are near Atlanta. My mom and brother and sister are here now—they're really my half-brother and half-sister, but I don't think of them that way. Christian and Leah. They're nine months and three weeks apart. Their dad—I still call him my step-dad—lives in Augusta. He and my mom got divorced a while back, and my mom got remarried.

"I lived with my mom for a while last year, sleeping on the couch, before I moved into these apartments. See, I went to recovery for three months. It was a place out in the country—my mom took me there after my boyfriend got busted in Augusta. And then after recovery, I came back to Atlanta and lived at her place so I didn't have to go back to the whole Augusta scene again. I just had to start my whole life over from scratch."

I remembered what Miss Kate told me before I left recovery. We were sitting in the office in that white clapboard house where all the women slept, and she looked at me and said, "We've taught you all we can here. I think you'll make it out there, but you need to stick to your meetings, and you're going to have to learn some humility."

I thought: "Humility? You've got to be kidding me. I've already been humiliated. I've humiliated myself for the past two years!" But she meant going out into the world and living clean and starting over with nothing. As for my meetings, I didn't stick to those. I basically thought I could make it on my own.

"I'm working really hard to get Paige back," I said to Brian Nichols now, sitting up straight on the vanity stool and putting my hands on my knees. "Completing recovery was one of the things the custody papers said I had to do. The other thing is to provide a stable home. And that's what I'm working toward now. I'm in school to be a medical assistant. I have two jobs. And now I've got this apartment." *Can't he see he has to let me keep going with this and get my daughter back? He can't just kill me and cut the whole thing off.*

"But, you know," I told him, "even though I'm closer to getting her back, I'm not ready for Paige yet. Financially I'm not ready. I mean, just this week my grandparents loaned me the money to move in here. I used to have a roommate, but living alone I needed help getting caught up with the bills."

I remembered my grandpa's voice on the phone when I called him—just days ago—and asked about the loan so I could move into this smaller, more affordable apartment on the other side of the complex. "Papa, I have something to ask you, and you can say no if you want to. I'll completely understand." My grandparents hadn't agreed to help me like this in years. They saw how my life had gone down after Mack. "Papa, I know there's no reason for you to trust me after all the lies, so you can say no." But he was listening to what I asked. He listened as I spoke, and then he asked about my grades. "I'm making A's," I told him. Then he said those words that totally shocked me: "Okay," he said, "we'll do it."

I took the picture frame off the counter again and held it in my lap. "And it's more than finances," I said to Brian Nichols. "I'm just not ready for Paige. If my aunt called me today and said, 'You can have her back,' I wouldn't take her."

He looked at me now, tilting his head to the side as if he didn't understand or thought I was nuts. *Okay. I've got him listening again.*

I tried to explain. I wanted him to feel where I was now as a mom—how painful it was, how much I still had left to do with Paige. "It's just that I've got to learn my child all over again. She's a new person. For two years I haven't been there—waking up with my child, giving her a bath, putting her to bed, taking her places. I only see her maybe once every few weeks, and I need to learn her again. I need to know her. There's so much I just don't know."

I sat back and looked at that picture frame. There I was, bending forward with my arm around a beautiful little girl, pulling her close. She was leaning against me and smiling. I was her mommy. She had her mommy with her. We were all together at my cousin's wedding—a family.

But who was that little girl? Who was she? I wanted to know so badly—everything about her. That's why I was working so hard. That's why I was hanging onto God for dear life. Fighting those drugs. Reading that book and trying to find my purpose. For her. To be with her. To deserve to be with her. And yet here I was, sitting in the bathroom of my apartment with this guy from the courthouse and all the guns and the lines of ice up on the counter. *Was it all for nothing, Lord? Is this where it ends? After all that's happened, am I going to miss out on knowing her? Won't I ever get to know who she's become?*

14 angel sent from god

"Do you want to see what drugs can do to you?" I asked him. I was smoking another cigarette, and suddenly, I thought I would show him my scar. I wanted him to really see what I had been through—to understand some of the consequences of my choices, so he could connect with me in my life a little more.

I also wanted him, when he looked at the scar, to say, "Wow, she's still here." If he could see that I had done bad things and survived—I mean, yes, I was paying the price, but I was still alive—then maybe he would start to believe he could have hope for himself. Some kind of hope. I figured his price was going to be heavy; at the very least he would be locked up for the rest of his life. But that was better than running and hurting more people. If he could just see that turning himself in was a good thing.

"Sure," he said. He was smoking now too.

"Well, here's what the drugs did to me." I put my cigarette down on the counter and lifted up the front of my tank top several inches above my belly button. I didn't think doing this was provocative; I just wanted to make a point. "See this scar?" It was a thick five-inch line running down the center of my torso from the lower part of my sternum to my belly button. At the bottom of the line and five inches out to each side was a round dot where an incision had been made.

"Yeah, that's pretty bad," he said.

"Well, I got it in a car accident." I pulled down my tank, picked up my cigarette again, and started smoking. "I had just seen my daughter at the doctor's office. And, you know, I was clean when I saw her. I wasn't messed up that morning. But when I got in the car, I started hearing voices like I was on those drugs. Psychosis, they call it. And so I heard this voice tell me to 'let go and let God.' And I was so freakin' crazy, I thought it was God telling me to let go of the steering wheel. 'I'm your child, God, so I can let go and close my eyes and when I open them, I'll be at the bottom of this hill because you'll take care of me.' Just nuts!

"So I let go and put my head back and closed my eyes. And the next time I opened them, it was two days later and I was in a hospital bed with two broken arms, three broken ribs, and a severed pancreas. That's what the scar's from. My car had gone across the median, off the road, and into a ditch. I probably should've been dead."

I took a drag on my cigarette now and crossed my legs, trying to hold his gaze and keep him with me. "And, you know, I was still so crazy after the accident that even when I was in the hospital I thought I was being monitored by hidden cameras—I actually thought I was in a foreign hospital. That's how deep it was. And I did *not* want to be in there. I just knew I didn't belong in that place. So one day after they took out my IV, I snuck out of the hospital and caught a cab."

He raised his eyebrows at that. *Okay, just keep listening here.*

"I used smoking as my way out. They were telling me, 'You're not supposed to be smoking.' And I would say, 'Y'all can't stop me from smoking.' So they would let me go outside and smoke at that point. Well, I came up with this plan to escape and catch a cab, so I walked outside this one day like I was just going to smoke. I had a tube hanging out of my nose and tubes coming out of my stomach to catch the fluids running out of me. And I went out there and hailed a cab and asked the guy to take me to my boyfriend's house. By then I had tucked the stomach tubes into my shorts, but I sure didn't look like I had any business leaving. Anyway, the cab took me, and when my boyfriend opened the front door and saw me there with the tube hanging out of my nose, he just freaked. He called my mom and they marched me right back up to that hospital. I don't even think anybody really knew I was gone."

I put out my cigarette now and looked more intently at Brian Nichols. If he could just get this and hear what I was saying. "The point is," I said, "those drugs almost destroyed me. And you know what? I used to want nothing to do with that stuff. I mean, ice used to be forbidden in my house. Right around the time Mack died and the drug first started getting big and people started bringing it over, I would say, 'Get that stuff out of here! Get that stuff out of my house!' But a year and a half later, I was weak, and I tried it, and that was it.

"I lost my daughter. And I told you my family put me in a mental hospital for three days—that was just before the accident. They thought I had lost my mind. *I* thought I had lost my mind. That's what those drugs did. Like I said, they ruined my life. I ruined my own life by doing them. And now I'm paying for it. But, man, at least I'm not dead. I'm working hard, trying to get my life on track. I'm still alive, and there's a reason for that. I just know there's a reason I'm still here."

Brian Nichols looked pretty mellow now. He wasn't moving. He was just sitting on top of the toilet staring off into space. I knew he'd been listening to me. But what was he thinking? I wanted him to see that he was still here for a reason too. He wasn't dead either. He was being given a chance to stop right now, and he needed to see that.

I decided to ask him something. Looking at him as he sat there quietly, I felt that he would answer me. I felt that he would be a little more open with me, now that I had just opened up my life to him. So I asked.

"Why did you choose me out of all the people in Atlanta?" I wanted some clue—something, anything—as to why this might be happening right now. "I mean, why me? Did you choose me randomly, or what?"

He sighed, and now he picked up his beer can. "Well, I just pulled up here, and I saw you come out of your house. And to be honest with you, I thought you were going for a booty call or something." *This is the most he's said in one breath in a long time.*

"A booty call?" *Please.* "Okay. So were you just going to wait for me to come back then?"

"Yeah," he answered. "A young female going out at two in the morning—that's what I thought you went out for, and I figured you'd have to come home some time. So I was going to wait. But then five minutes later I see you pulling back around, and I'm like, 'She must've gone to the store.'" *So he was going to wait for me no matter what. He targeted me. That's terrifying.*

"Yeah," I said. "I was going out for cigarettes. But, I mean, that was it? That was how you chose me?"

"Yeah," he said, taking a swig of his beer.

"Well, why'd you choose Bridgewater Apartments? I mean, there must be four or five other apartment complexes right in this same area. Why this one?" I was thinking about the complex and where it was located—it wasn't right off the highway or anything. Assuming he was going north from downtown on I-85, he would've gotten off at Beaver Ruin Road, then taken a left at the first light, a right two lights later onto Satellite Boulevard, and then finally a left into this apartment complex. That seemed pretty elaborate to me. And how many miles was it to this place from the Fulton County Courthouse? It had to be at least twenty miles. *Why here? How in the world did he end up here?*

"I guess randomly," he said. "I was just driving around. Maybe I just got led here by something, you know."

But this was a big apartment complex. I lived basically in the very back of my section, and I supposed it made sense that he would swing around somewhere in the back; but still, it was a big complex. He had to take two rights and a left once he got inside the complex to get here—that was three turns. And why did he choose my apartment at that time—the moment I was walking out the door? And an apartment I had just moved into? And why did my grandparents decide to loan me that money earlier in the week? And why did the leasing office assign me to this particular apartment, not some other one? I didn't get it, and as I sat there on the vanity stool, it started to dawn on me that maybe this was God.

Right then I could feel a rush of heat through my whole body. *Maybe there really is some purpose in this guy being here.* There was no other way to explain it. God knew I would be here in this apartment. He knew I would be walking out for cigarettes at 2:00 a.m. He knew Brian Nichols would be pulling up when I left. He knew it all, and he was in control right now. I felt shocked, almost like I couldn't move. Maybe God really did *bring* this guy here for some reason.

"Do you believe in miracles?" I asked Brian Nichols again. He had said yes the first time, but I wanted him to get this point right here. I mean, I believed in miracles, but I had never really *lived* one like this before. Or maybe I had—like living through my car accident and surviving all those drugs. And Paige was a miracle child to me after her premature birth. But I had never really recognized a miracle like this right when it was happening to me, right when it was all unfolding. I needed Brian Nichols to see what I was seeing. This was really, really big.

"Don't you see that it's just a total miracle that you're in this apartment?" I asked him. "I mean, you could be anywhere. You could be running. You could be dead. But you're alive and sitting in here with me right now—in an apartment I just moved into two days ago. And you pull up in here just as I happen to be going out? That's crazy. How do you explain it? It had to be God. It's like he must want you to be here or something. What else do you think could've led you to my doorstep?"

He set his beer down on the floor again. I could see some emotion come up in his eyes, some—was it?—passion. *Is he seeing it, God? Does he get it? Is this you working right here and helping me? Because if this is you doing this—if there's a purpose for him being here—then that means you're really with me right now. You're really here. You're really going to help me. Please keep helping me.*

Then Brian Nichols answered.

"I don't know," he said, looking me in the eye, squinting as if he was trying to figure something out. "I don't know. I mean, maybe you're my angel sent from God. Maybe that's what this is. Maybe he led me right to you."

15 do you mind if i read?

Do you have anything I can eat?" Brian Nichols asked. *Is he actually asking me for food now? First his laundry. Now food. This is good. I know him asking me like this is good.*

I was still thinking about what he had just said—about me being an angel and God leading him here to my apartment. I was no angel, but I knew I had to be getting through to him. Had to be. Something in his eyes made him look like he was getting it—what I was seeing. Like he believed it too. That there was a reason for all of this. A purpose and everything. It was as if God really was working here and answering my prayers. It just continued to blow me away right then.

I remembered feeling the same way when my grandparents agreed to loan me that money earlier in the week. That was on Monday. The day before, on Sunday, I was sitting in church in Dacula with my Uncle David's family—the same church where I was supposed to meet Paige in the morning—with thirty dollars in my pocketbook, not knowing how I was going to pay the bills or anything, not knowing where I was going to live. And as I was sitting there, I thought, "Lord, I know you have a plan for me. Just tell me what it is. I don't know how I'm going to pay my bills, but I know if I keep trying to do your will, then you'll provide for me somehow."

Right then I decided to give half of my thirty dollars to God—just on blind faith—so I dropped fifteen bucks in the offering plate. By doing that I was trying to say, "Look, God, I trust you." I just wanted some way to show him. Then, the very next day my grandparents agreed to loan me the money. I didn't know if there was a connection between their decision and my putting fifteen bucks in the offering, but somehow I could see the Lord was working in my life. It was like he was rewarding me for being faithful. I was seeing results. I still had the dark secret of my drug addiction; I was still battling that. But God was showing me, "Look, Ashley, I really am real, okay?"

I looked at Brian Nichols now and tried to remember what food was in my cabinets. *You're really real, God. I'm getting it. Just stay with me.* "Sure, we can look," I said. "I mean, I don't have much, but let's see." Actually, I had just been to the store, but I still didn't have a lot.

He stood up, walked out of the bathroom, and waited for me in the hallway. As I got up from the vanity stool, I glanced over at the guns again. *Well, at least he hasn't picked those up in a while. Let's just keep it that way, God. I've got to keep working the trust thing with this guy. He's just got to let me walk out of here, and that's all there is to it. I'm walking out of this apartment in the morning. I'm leaving at 9:30, and I'm going to see Paige.*

I passed Brian Nichols and walked into the living room. Coming out of that small hallway just to my right was the glass-top column table my mom had given me when I moved out of her place into my old apartment. The thermostat was right above that table—it was low so someone in a wheelchair could reach it, I figured. On the table I had set up some Reader's Digest books between two gold angel bookends from Aunt Kim's house; the colors in the book bindings—burgundy, yellow, and blue—matched the rug under my coffee table to the left. Walking by now, I noticed that my silver cell phone was sitting there in front of those books. Okay. At least now I knew where it was.

Brian Nichols followed right behind me as I walked over to the kitchen. To my right was the dining area. My queen-sized mattress and box springs from my other apartment—it was a two-bedroom place—were propped up against the wall next to the column table;

and there was still just enough room for my table and chairs. I didn't have a real dining room set because the guy who'd been living with me had taken his back, so in this place I was using my outdoor table and chairs. The table was tall, not very big, with a wrought iron base and a glass top. The two wrought iron chairs with cream-colored cushions were tall, too, like bar stools. The iron was starting to rust and chip from having been outside on the patio at my old apartment.

I walked into the kitchen, passing the fridge on my right, and went directly across the room to the cabinets just to the right of the stove. I kept dry things like chips, cereal bars, bread, and pasta in there.

"Go ahead and look," I said to him, opening the cabinets and stepping back. "I don't have much in here." The overhead light was still on, and so was the small ceramic lamp next to the sink behind me.

Mostly what I had on the shelves were canned goods and boxed items. I had some cookies, but I didn't have many other snacks—at least, not fattening stuff—because I was always feeling chubby and battling my weight. In my world right then, anything more than 120 pounds was chubby. And since I wasn't doing ice all that much—on ice I could go days and hardly eat and not even notice—keeping the pounds off was harder.

I thought back to high school and all the exercising I did to stay skinny. *How on earth did I do that?* There was the half hour of aerobics I did in my room before school; the time after school in the gym with Uncle David or, if it was basketball season, at practice; then the two miles I would run up and down the hills in our neighborhood every night after cooking dinner and cleaning up. I hated it, the whole battle against my weight, but I couldn't break out of it. Even now I was in it. Just a couple of weeks ago I had called that guy I knew to bring me some ice so I could drop a few pounds. "Just let him be there this one time," I had prayed—that awful thing I did with God. It was horrible, that back and forth. *Thank you, God. Thank you that I'm done with that junk now and all of that is over.*

As Brian Nichols stood there looking in my kitchen cabinet, I glanced over at the microwave sitting on the counter to my right. The clock read 3:30. *3:30? So we've only been in here for an hour and a half? That can't be right.* I'd burned enough energy in that amount of time to last me for days. If it was 3:30, then I had six more hours with this guy before I left to go see Paige. *Wow. That's a freakin' eternity.* But I *was* going to see Paige. It was happening. I had to keep picturing it. I looked to the left of the microwave at a framed black-and-white photograph of Paige standing on the beach. *See, Ashley, it's a good thing you unpacked everything and obsessed over putting things where they're supposed to be, or Paige wouldn't be all over this apartment for this guy to see right now.*

I started thinking back over the day I had just had on Friday. I had missed my devotion that morning—how had that happened? Let's see. I had snorted ice late Thursday afternoon and stayed up moving and unpacking until dawn. Then, after I finally fell asleep early Friday morning, my step-dad called and woke me up before lunch, talking about the guy standing here in my kitchen right now. *That's insane. Just nuts that this is happening.* And then I jumped into my day. I went to work at the restaurant. And I forgot to do my devotion—the first time I had missed since February 7, when I put that dollar bill in the offering at Aunt Kim's church for my copy of *The Purpose-Driven Life*.

I mean, with the move and everything, it would have been easy to get confused about my routine, but even that wasn't like me. I just didn't miss my time with God. It didn't happen. Not since February 7. Not since I realized my life had to change or else. Even though I was fighting the drugs, I still woke up every morning and read a chapter in my Bible somewhere—I just opened the Bible and picked out a chapter at random. And then I read a chapter in my *Purpose-Driven Life*. My mindset was, "I don't care if I have to be at work in thirty minutes—it doesn't matter, okay, Ashley? Because if you don't start your day reading this, it's just going to get worse. So you might as well be late for work because you've got to get something out of what God's trying to tell you right here."

I highlighted and took notes in the book, and I kept a journal of the things that spoke to me—I copied right out of the book. And I would call Aunt Kim and say, "This is what I read in *The Purpose-*

Driven Life today, and this is what it means to me." If nothing else good happened in my life, at least I was going to hear God every day. That was my thinking. I was hanging on for dear life trying to trust God—trusting him to make me a good mother; to send me some Christian friends; to guide my life; to fix my relationships with my family; to help me fight those drugs. And I needed something from God every day, or I just wasn't going to make it. Every time I started my devotion I invited God in to speak to me. I prayed, "Jesus, come in and show me what to do." And it was working. I could feel peace all through that old apartment. I didn't have a roommate, so there was no drama. There was just this peace. It was as if God just completely filled my whole heart.

Now here I was, standing in the kitchen with Brian Nichols, and I thought, "Man, if there was ever a day—I mean *ever* a day—I needed God to speak to me, it's today. And I forgot to do my devotion. That's crazy. That's just nuts. How could I have missed that?"

Suddenly it occurred to me that I should just go ahead and do my devotion right then. I had been saying I was done cheating God out of his time, so why not go ahead and give him his time now? I mean, things seemed to be moving in my favor here somewhat, but who really knew how this night was going to end. Only God knew if I was going to make it. And I thought, "Okay. If there's a chance I'm going to leave this earth tonight, then at least I want to have that next chapter of *Purpose-Driven Life* under me."

"Hey, Matt," I said. *Wait, is that his name? What's his name? Think, Ashley. Snap out of it. What did the TV say his name was?* "Brian. Hey, Brian, do you mind if I read?"

He didn't seem to notice that slip—either that or he didn't care; and right then I realized this was the first time I had called Brian Nichols by his first name all night. *Brian.* Saying it that first time felt strange. I mean, the guy had held me at gunpoint. I was his hostage. He had killed three people at the courthouse just today. But I figured

I was trying to talk to him normally, so I guessed it made sense that I should start using his name.

Brian closed the cabinets now and stepped back. *I guess nothing in there appealed to him.* I couldn't have eaten right then for a million dollars.

"What do you want to read?" he asked.

"It's just a book," I said, pointing toward the hallway. "It's back in my room."

"Okay," he said. "Yeah, sure." *He's starting to let me do what I want. This is very, very good.*

I walked back across the living room, with Brian following me again, passing his red jacket on the small bench in the hallway on the way into my bedroom. *And he's following me around the house like he's my guest or something and I'm the host. Just let it stay this way, God. Let's keep going with this.*

I went over to the dresser in front of the windows and grabbed *The Purpose-Driven Life* and my Bible from out of my wicker basket. Those two books always sat on the top. The bright light from my closet was enough to read by, so I didn't bother with the gold lamp sitting on the dresser next to the basket. I just sat down with my books on the end of the bed, on the side closest to the windows. And Brian sat down right next to me.

For a minute I didn't know what to think about him sitting so close. I didn't feel threatened. I didn't think there was anything like rape going through his mind. He had already taped and tied me up and carried me across the hall, and he was a lot closer to me then than he was now. And with the whole shower thing, I thought he probably would've raped me by now if he was going to do that. I wasn't sure, but I wasn't as worried about it right this minute.

Actually, I thought maybe he was sitting with me like this because he might be starting to trust me. Or because he felt closer to me after everything I had told him in the bathroom. Or because he just felt sad. He still seemed very toned down—as he said, he had had a long day—and who knew what was going through his mind? I had no idea where he had been, what he had done. Whatever was happening, something was changing between us—that seemed clear.

I took my Bible—the black leather one from my grandpa—out from underneath my book and laid it on the bed. Then I opened up my *Purpose-Driven Life* on my lap. I was using a paper bookmark Paige had colored at Sunday school. It read "Jesus is coming again!" There was a big cross on it that she had colored brown. The rest of the bookmark was yellow and green and blue and red and purple and orange. Paige had used scissors to cut a fringe all around the edges, and right at the cross she had almost cut the bookmark in two.

I turned in my book now to where the marker was—I was on Day 32, "Using What God Gave You"—and I looked over at Brian. *Did he see what the marker said about Jesus?* Maybe he would think about Jesus and feel some hope.

"Do you want to hear it?" I asked him.

"Sure," he said. "You can read it out loud."

So I began.

16 what do you think mine is?

This was not my first time to read *The Purpose-Driven Life*. I had tried twice before, the first time being last summer, right after I started using ice again. I had been out of recovery for a few months. Finally, I had saved enough money cleaning houses to buy this piece of junk for a car—not the same one I had now—so I could go see Paige back in Augusta. And as soon as I got there, I went right back to the old crowd. "I'm not crazy anymore, you guys!" I told them. But my weight was bothering me again, and I felt an urge to get messed up. No big deal, I thought. I could control it now. And then my old boyfriend, John, was back and I wanted to get closer to him, so I just went back to doing what we used to do. Not as much as before. And I snorted—I didn't hot rail. But it just wasn't a good thing at all.

On one of those trips home, I stopped by my step-dad's place. Even though my mom was remarried to another man now, my step-dad was still very important in my life. He still lived in the same house where I had spent my teenage years. He was the father of my brother and sister. I loved him. We were in touch often, and I still went to see him. When I stopped by this one time, I saw a copy of *The Purpose-Driven Life* out on the coffee table—Aunt Kim had given it to him for Father's Day.

"Are you reading this?" I asked him. Something about the book just drew me, which was a big deal because I didn't read books much then.

"No," he said, so I told him I would take it home with me.

Right away I went back to Atlanta—I had moved out of my mom's place and into my first apartment—and I started reading. But after doing seventeen days of a chapter-a-day, I started missing days and trying to pick back up where I left off. "Oh, just forget it," I thought. "I'm not doing this right now. This is not the way the book is supposed to be read. I'll do it later." That was July.

Then the guy from Augusta—whose pants were left hanging in my closet for Brian Nichols—moved up and started sharing my apartment with me. I was doing a lot of ice then, but I started the book again in the fall, maybe in September. And I actually made it through all forty chapters. I was probably high or confused a lot of the time I was reading, but I fought to hang onto God too. It was like I was trying to have it both ways, keeping God over here and the drugs over there. I would read *The Purpose-Driven Life* and then go do drugs up my nose. God must've been looking at me, going, "What a hypocrite!" Anyway, I read the whole book, and it might have opened up some doors in my thinking; but it didn't really register with me then. Once I finished it, I sent the book to John.

Then came February 7, with God pounding at my door, saying, "Ashley, you can stop; I'm here," and Satan whispering in my ear, "It's okay." And all of the back and forth with that guy on the phone. *Let him answer. Don't let him answer.* Just, basically, spiritual warfare, as Brian Nichols said. As Aunt Kim said. God and Satan fighting. The drugs had a hold on me, and something had to be done.

So now I was all the way to Day 32 in my book, and since I was about to do today's chapter, I was counting it as if I hadn't missed a day yet. I started reading to Brian while we were sitting on my bed, beginning with the Bible verse at the head of the chapter "Using What God Gave You":

"'Since we find ourselves fashioned into all these excellently formed and marvelously functioning parts in Christ's body, let's just go ahead and be what we were made to be. Romans 12:5.'"

Then:

"'What you are is God's gift to you; what you do with yourself is your gift to God. Danish proverb.'"

Then I read the first page of the chapter:

"'God deserves your best. He shaped you for a purpose, and he expects you to make the most of what you have been given. He doesn't want you to worry about or covet abilities you don't have. Instead he wants you to focus on talents he has given you to use. When you attempt to serve God in ways you're not shaped to serve, it feels like forcing a square peg into a round hole. It's frustrating and produces limited results. It also wastes your time, your talent, and your energy. The best use of your life is to serve God out of your shape. To do this you must discover your shape, learn to accept and enjoy it, and then develop it to its fullest potential.'"

"Stop," Brian said suddenly. I looked over at him; I was about to turn the page. "Read that again."

This must be speaking to him. He's got some religious background, and if he's anything like me, he's fighting for it right now. God, you just speak to him right here.

"Okay," I said. "I'll read it again." So I started: "'God deserves your best,'" and I reread the rest of that first page.

Brian was rubbing his hands over his knees now. "So," he said, "what do you think your purpose is?" *This is interesting. He wanted me to read it again. Now he wants to talk?*

"Well," I said, taking a deep breath, "I think it's to serve others, help others. And to serve God—you know, be his servant and spread his Word."

All right, if he wants to have a discussion, I might as well ask him too. "What do *you* think?" I asked, watching him out of the corner of my eye.

He paused. Then he answered in that low tone. "I think it's to talk to people and tell them about what's happened to you." *Wait, is he telling me* my *purpose—what he thinks* I *should do? He sure doesn't know me that well to be telling me my purpose.*

But then I thought, "Maybe there's something to what he said. I mean, I've been doing that all night—talking to him and telling him what's happened to me."

Then he asked, "What do you think mine is?" *Okay. He told me my purpose, so now I get to tell him his. This is really just incredible.*

"I don't know," I said. Was I about to say this? Yes. I had to say this. "Maybe it's to minister to people in prison." I waited. He was quiet. I could hear him breathing. His hands were still.

Nothing for a few seconds. Then almost a whisper. "What do you think I should do?" he asked.

I could see he was looking at the floor. *Okay, God. This is it. I'm telling him. This is an open door. Help me just say it all straight. Help me say it right. This is your thing right here.*

"Look," I said, putting the book aside and turning to him, "you've got to turn yourself in. You've got to stop running. You've got to pay for what you did. You killed some people. You've got to pay for that."

Brian was still looking down.

"You know," I continued, "I did a bunch of drugs—I'm an addict. And now I don't have Paige with me. So I'm paying for my mistakes. I used ice because I was scared to death after Mack died. I wasn't big enough to face the situation. So I used ice, and now I don't have my little girl. I'm paying. We all have to pay."

He wasn't saying anything, wasn't responding at all. *Is he getting this? Is he angry? Is this too much?* But I felt bold right then. Like I could keep talking and say what was on my heart. He had to pay, but I wanted him to have some hope too. Without hope he might not turn himself in. So I just kept going with it.

"And, you know, I'm saying all that about having to pay, and we do have to pay for what we do. I mean, when we take an action, we're accepting responsibility for that action. But God also forgives us. The Bible says we can come to him—you know, come to our heavenly Father and ask and really mean it—and he'll forgive us our sins. No matter what you've done, it's like, God can still forgive you. You've got to believe that."

I was thinking back to a Bible verse I had read once about God being a father to the fatherless. There were all those years I didn't have my daddy, but when I read that verse, I thought, "Look, here's the Father I need." And I heard God say to me then, "I love you, Ashley. I've forgiven you. I've been knocking at your door for a long time."

Looking down at my hands in my lap now, I wanted to take things with Brian a little further. I wanted to equalize things between us—to get him to see that we were the same in God's eyes. He had to see in his mind, "She's the same as me," so he could get this point right here.

I tucked my hair behind my ears and closed my eyes, and I tried to remember how I had heard Aunt Kim say this; she'd said it to me so many times, I almost felt as if her words were coming out of me. *God, help me say this right.*

"I mean, what I understand is that sin is sin," I said. "God's looking at it all the same way. The world may not see it all the same way, but God does. He doesn't say, like, 'Okay, you can't go out and kill people, but it's fine if you come over here and lie to your wife.' Do you see what I'm saying? What you've done—I mean, yes, it's really terrible, and I know firsthand because someone killed my husband—and you've got to pay. But to God it's no different than what I've done by lying to my family or doing drugs or stealing from a department store or cheating on my boyfriend. It's no different, dude. Not to God. And if he can forgive me, he can forgive you."

Was he getting it? Did I say all of that right? He just had to see there was some hope. Even if he was locked up forever, there was hope. *How could I get it across better?*

I remembered something one of the women had told me at recovery. I was doing my fifth step with her: you had to admit your wrongs to another person. And after I'd been talking with her one day in the house after a meeting, she said, "You sound to me like you're trying to be perfect for your family, but you know, you can't be perfect. You'll never be perfect." Then she said something I would never forget. And I said it to Brian now.

"If God wanted us to be perfect, Brian, he would've put us up there on that cross instead of Jesus." I was pointing at the ceiling now, trying to get him to see what I was seeing. "Look, I'm not perfect. If I was perfect, I'd be Jesus himself. God knows we're not perfect—we're sinners. That doesn't mean we don't pay for what we've done and try to change and make things right. But it means we need forgiveness. And we've got to ask God for it. We can ask him, and he'll give it to us."

I had no idea how Brian was taking any of this. He could've been thinking, "Look, I just wish you'd shut up, okay?" But I didn't think that was it. I was facing him now on the bed. He wasn't looking at me—he was looking straight ahead at my tall dresser with that picture of Paige on it—but there was something about the way he was listening as I talked: He would look down, then look back up at the dresser, then down at his hands in his lap. I just thought he was with me—it seemed like his mind was working. He wasn't all glazed over as if he had checked out or something. He didn't look mad. Maybe he was—I didn't know. All I knew was that I was going to keep working hard to get through to this guy. I was leaving to go see Paige in the morning. I was walking out of this apartment at 9:30, and he had to turn himself in and stop hurting people.

"Look, you never know what God might have for you to do in prison," I said, trying to go back to what he asked about his purpose. "You don't know what could happen for you in there. My boyfriend in Augusta—he and I were strung out on ice together and doing all that crazy stuff; and he did all kinds of bad things. Illegal things. And now he's locked up for it. He's paying for what he did. But, you know, he's been starting to write me these letters saying he's sorry for what he did and how God is working in his life now. And to me he sounds like a totally different person. So, you know what? There's hope. Wherever you are, there's hope. I mean, I'm seeing it right now happen for someone I know."

At that moment Brian stood up. He didn't say anything. Didn't look at me. Just stared straight ahead like he was looking right through that dresser, right through the wall. *Maybe I've pushed this too far.* I tried to think back over what all I had just said to him. I was pretty tough. He asked me what I thought he should do, and I told him. I didn't hold back. *I thought it was okay, God. I was just going with it. Trying to give this guy some hope so he would have the guts to do the right thing.* I really hoped I hadn't just blown what God was trying to do in here. *He's got to turn himself in. There's no other option. Not any good one.*

Looking up at Brian now, I couldn't read him. Couldn't read him at all. All I had to go on was his profile. I couldn't see his eyes. He just stood there. Not moving. So I waited. *What's he going to do?*

Then he turned and walked out of the room.

17 learning me

I leaned forward on the bed to see where he was going. He was walking across the hall to the bathroom. *What's he doing? Those guns are in there.*

Standing up now, I moved toward my bedroom door so I could watch him. He was bent down over the counter near those lines. Then I heard that inhale again; he had snorted another one. *Well, God, you've kept him from acting crazy on that stuff till now, so could you give me another break and keep him chilled out this time too?* For a beginner, two of those lines seemed like a whole lot to be doing.

"Hey," Brian said, standing up and turning toward the door to look at me across the hall. "Come in here."

I was not looking forward to this. I hated that those drugs were in there, and I hated that he was doing them again. But I walked across the hall to the bathroom as he asked and stood in the doorway.

"I just want you to know something," he said, sniffing a little to get the rest of the ice up his nose. He turned and faced me in that tight tee shirt and those high waters as if he was about to come at me for a tackle.

"Yeah," I said, "what?"

"You know, I'm still in control here."

He just stood there looking at me. I guessed he was waiting for my response.

"Okay," I answered him. "That's fine." *Yeah right, dude. If you're still in control, then why are you following me around my house and asking me to use my washing machine? You're supposed to be holding me hostage here, and you're going around asking me for stuff. But, sure, you can be in control if you want.*

As I saw it, he could try and convince himself all night that he was still in control. I had no problem with that. Fine. I'd agree with him. *Go on. I'll say whatever you want to hear.* He just wasn't going to convince me so easily. I mean, I wasn't stupid. He was a big guy, and for all I knew he could turn on a dime and start sticking those guns up in my face again. But the thing was, now I saw who really was in control. And it wasn't Brian Nichols. It wasn't me, either. It was God.

I stepped back into the hall to get out of his way as he walked by me, and I saw my clogs on the floor near the bench where his red jacket was lying. He must've put my shoes there; I had no idea why. My cigarettes, the lighter, and the ashtray were over on the counter in the bathroom, so I went and grabbed those quickly. Then I followed Brian into the living room.

He was standing between the dining and living areas, looking around. After a second or two he went and sat down on the brown leather sofa against the wall to my left. That was a piece of furniture the guy who lived with me had left behind, and sitting up on the back of it was that big mirror I hadn't gotten around to hanging yet. The wood coffee table with a light gray, mosaic tile top belonged to the same guy. The patchwork rug in front of the sofa was mine; so were the two cherry end tables on either side of the sofa and the matching lamps. Next to the lamps on each table I had set a pillar candle. I always liked to keep things evened out.

Wanting to keep an eye on Brian, I walked directly across the room to the long bar separating the kitchen from the living area. The bright overhead light in the kitchen and that little lamp by the sink were the only lights on in this part of the house. I turned and faced Brian where he was sitting on the far left side of the sofa, and I leaned on the end of the bar—it was more like a long half-wall with a ledge about eight inches wide—pushing aside a big silver picture frame of Paige so I didn't knock it down. I put the ashtray, lighter, and my cigarettes next to the picture on the ledge.

"So," he asked, crossing a leg over one knee. "What do you like to do?"

What do I like to do? I guess he's really trying to learn me here. Well, I'm all for it. I'll just keep opening up my life to him. "I like to make things," I said. "And fix things and paint and all that kind of stuff. You know, artsy stuff." I pointed toward the front of the living room, to his left, where Paige's massive, solid wood toy box was sitting in front of my long, skinny picture table and two windows.

"I painted that toy box right there. A friend of mine made it and I painted it." The toy box had every color on it that I could find. I had painted checks on the sides and thick diagonal stripes on the top. I really didn't know how that one guy and I ever moved the box in here. Even when it was empty I had to get on the floor and push it with my feet.

"And I covered this bench right here." Now I was pointing down at a whitewashed bench with pedestal feet right in front of the bar. For the cushion I had chosen this sort of fancy beige fabric with textured swirls.

"And you know all that white furniture in my bedroom?" He nodded. "I painted all that—the dressers and nightstands. And I spray-painted the hardware. I'm going to paint that room a summer green.

"Actually," I said, "I'm planning to paint all the rooms in here. See, in my old apartment I had color everywhere. I painted my dining room red. My bedroom was this golden straw color, and everything I put in that room, like my comforter and stuff, was burgundy. And then the bathroom—well—that took me two weeks. I was painting these burgundy-and-gold stripes on the walls using a ruler to draw them, and it just took me forever."

I pulled out a cigarette now and lit it, laying the pack and lighter back on the bar.

"You sure do smoke a lot," he said suddenly. *Well, that takes some nerve, dude, after you just snorted that line in there.*

I rolled my eyes. "Believe me, after all the dope and stuff I've done, smoking's not the worst thing I could do."

I took a long drag and looked over at that big eight-by-ten of Paige in the silver frame next to the ashtray. She was maybe three years old there. It was her school picture for Mother's Day Out. They had her sitting against a white backdrop and holding a white rose. She was looking down at it, and she looked kind of sad. She was still living with me then, and my mom told me that her little face was starting to wear the same expression as mine. And I was sad—man, was I sad and miserable.

"You know," I told Brian, "I really wanted to go to decorating school when I first moved here to Atlanta—that was my plan. But my mom's husband discouraged me. He said there were so many interior decorators here, I'd never make it. So I tossed that idea. That's why I'm in medical assistant school now. I figure I can go into sports medicine and get a good-paying job and support Paige that way. You know, have a career."

Brian just sat on the couch, watching me and listening. He didn't interrupt. He seemed to be paying attention to what I was telling him and maybe getting to know me a little bit. It was as if he had never gone in there and snorted that second line. He was just as chilled out as before. And still pretty melancholy. He was probably just completely wiped out. Who knew how many hours he'd been awake in jail before he killed those people and started running?

"Mack and I," I began again—I was just going to talk the guy's ears off if he would let me. Whatever it took. Because I was walking out that door at 9:30. I was getting out of this apartment. "Well, Mack—he had a remodeling business. He was really, really good at it."

I never saw this highway sign. I was too busy working and moving on March 11 to pay much attention to the news—to my step-dad's great dismay.

I did see Brian Nichols's mug shot (left) on TV. But when he held me at gunpoint and told me who he was, I couldn't remember it.

My first interview after being held hostage (right). By the emotion on my face, I probably just finished talking about my young daughter Paige.

My first-grade picture, 1983. Augusta Christian Schools. Mom, Aunt Kim, and Uncle David all worked there; my grandpa was the former headmaster.

Here's my basketball picture, junior year at Lakeside High School—before I started using drugs. Pot smoking started the next summer. It was all downhill from there.

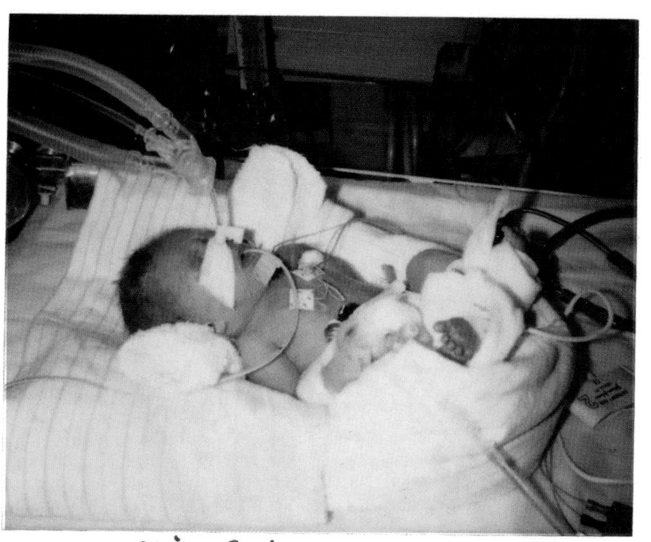

The first time I saw Paige was in this Polaroid, taken right after she was born prematurely and put into the special-care nursery. She was fighting for her life. I cried and cried.

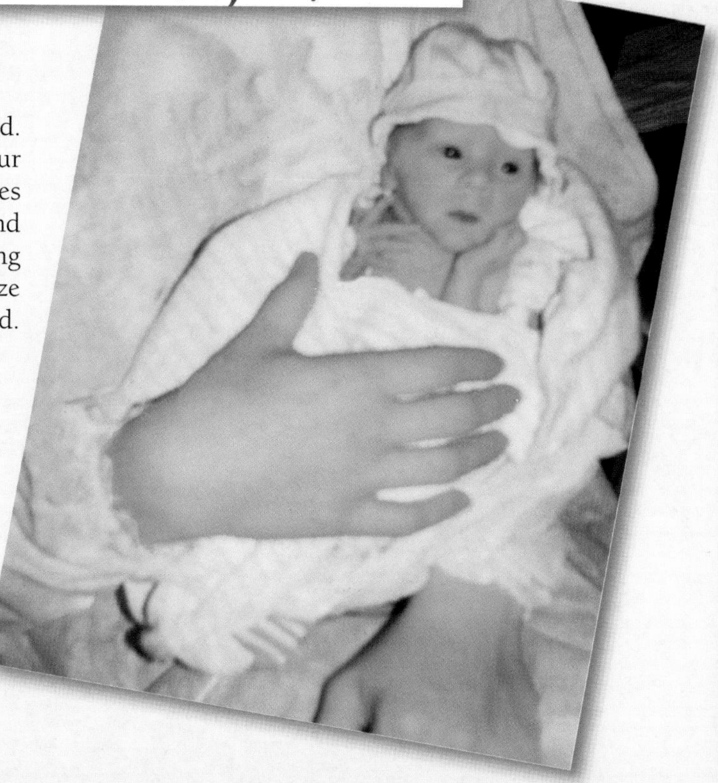

Paige coming around. We had to wash our hands for two minutes and put on robes and masks before holding her. She was the size of my hand.

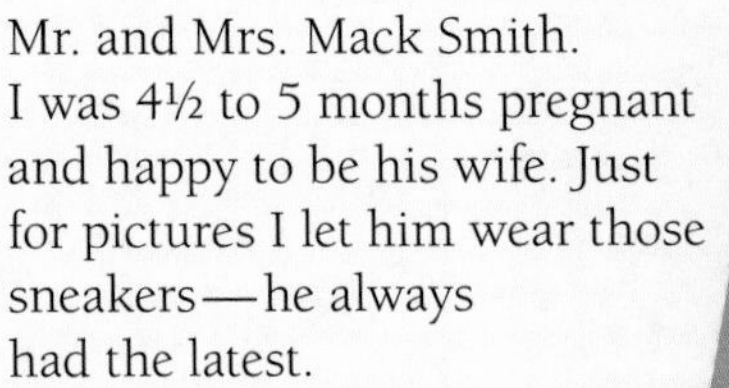

Mr. and Mrs. Mack Smith. I was 4½ to 5 months pregnant and happy to be his wife. Just for pictures I let him wear those sneakers—he always had the latest.

Our wedding reception. He slammed the cake in my face. I knew it was coming—we were having fun here!

Two lives, two hearts
joined together in friendship
united forever in love.
It is with joy that we,
Elizabeth Ashley Copeland
and
Daniel McFarland Smith, Jr.
invite you to share
in a celebration of love
as we exchange our marriage vows
on Sunday, the fourteenth of March
Nineteen hundred and ninety-nine
at four-thirty in the afternoon
Augusta Richmond County Civic Center
Augusta, Georgia

Mack

Ashley

Our wedding invitation. We loved it.

Mack and me on a Friday night (above). We were getting ready to go out. Probably in a limo with our friends. Not good.

Strung out on ice, 2003 (above). My friend snapped the picture, saying, "You're gonna thank me for this." She wanted me to see how bad I looked: skinny, delirious, unable to produce a real smile. Sad.

Mack and me with our best friends, Mike and Katie—Mack's nephew and his wife. New Year's Eve 2000. This was taken just before we went to the club where Mack knocked me out cold and left me lying on the sidewalk.

New parents. My husband Mack and me a few days after Paige was born (above). Man, were we young—21 and 20! May 1999.

Above: Mack looking mad and me trying to humor him. Not unusual. Summer 1998. We had just started dating. I got pregnant a few months later.

Christmas 2000. Aunt Kim had taken me Christmas shopping in Atlanta. Mack loved Abercrombie & Fitch—he was all about brand names.

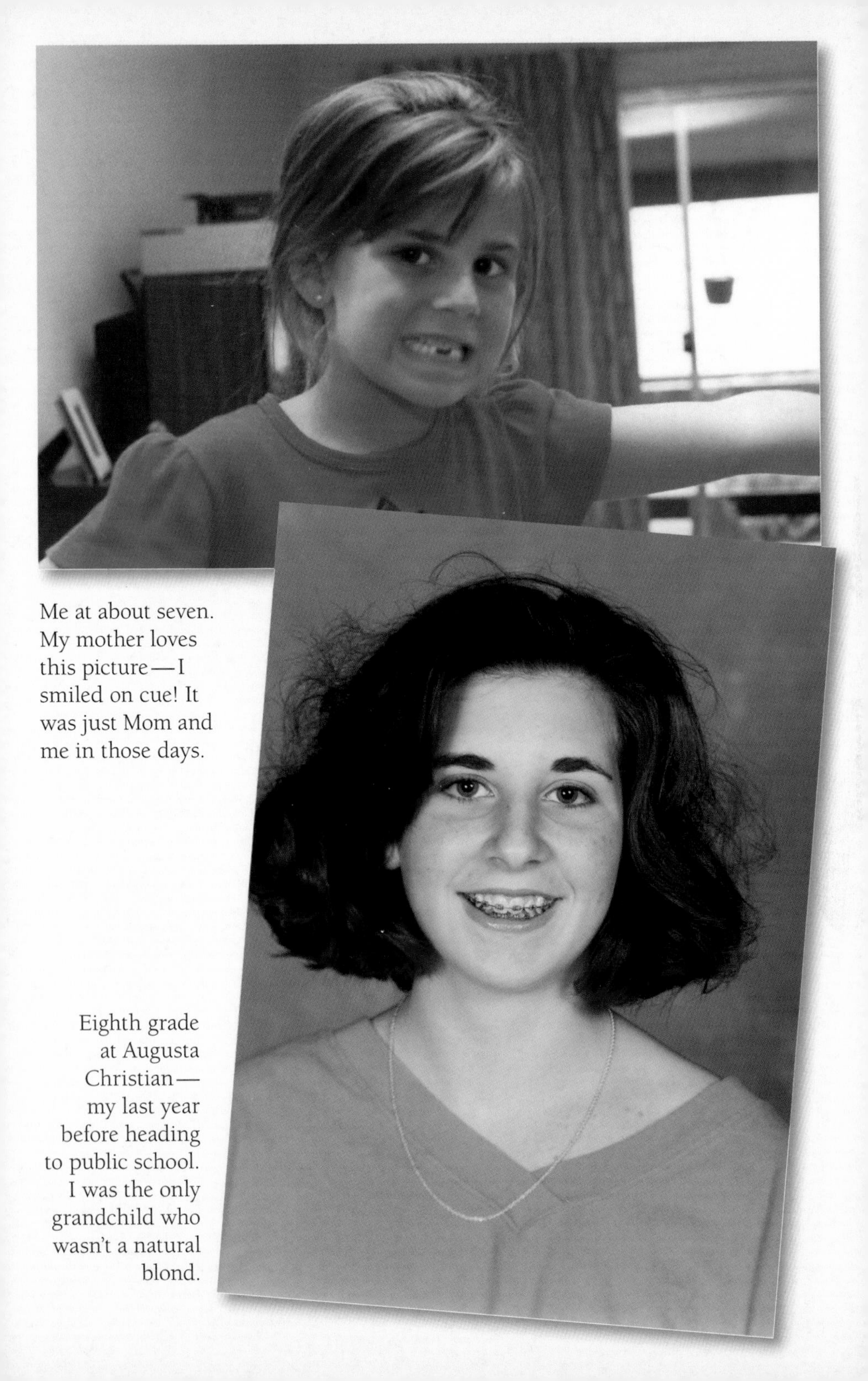

Me at about seven. My mother loves this picture — I smiled on cue! It was just Mom and me in those days.

Eighth grade at Augusta Christian — my last year before heading to public school. I was the only grandchild who wasn't a natural blond.

Miracle baby. Angel child. Me at age 20 holding Paige a few weeks after she was born. I practically lived at that hospital and drove those nurses crazy.

Daddy snuck home from work to catch a quick cat-nap and hold the new love of his life.

Our first Easter as a family, 2000. We vowed to take a family picture every Easter—but we only had one more together.

My favorite picture of Mack. Tan, content, sitting outside, where he liked to be most. April 2000.

Mr. Mack Smith
Carpenter

MARTINEZ, Ga. - Mr. Mack Smith, 23, of Martinez, loving husband of Mrs. Ashley Smith, died Saturday, August 18, 2001.

Funeral services will be held at noon, Wednesday, August 22, 2001, at Platt's Funeral Home, Evans, with Reverend Terry Doss from Warren Baptist Church officiating. Burial will follow at Bellevue Memorial Gardens.

Additional survivors include his parents, Mr. and Mrs. Dan (Cindy) Smith of Appling; his daughter, Miss Paige Smith of Martinez; three brothers, Mr. Dennis Smith of Augusta, Mr. Joel Smith of Appling and Mr. Bill Smith of Grovetown; one sister, Ms. Jeanne Smith of Appling; and two nephews, Mike and Denny Smith.

A lifelong resident of Columbia County, Mack attended Harlem Middle and Harlem High School and was the owner of Mack Smith Construction Co. He was a devoted son, husband and father.

Pallbearers for the service will be Taylor Hardy, Mark Smith, Carl Roland, Shaun Minyard, J.P. Holland and Steven Newman.

If so desired, memorials may be made to the Morgan Paige Smith Memorial Fund.

The family will receive friends at the funeral home on Tuesday from 7 to 9 p.m.

Platt's Funeral Home, 337 N. Belair Road, Evans. 706-860-6166.

The Augusta Chronicle-August 21, 2001

Mack's death announcement. I was in a total Xanax haze writing this and making the funeral arrangements.

Mack holding his "best buddy"—his spitting image with that pug nose! I showed this to Brian Nichols after telling him what happened to Mack. I wanted him to feel my loss.

CERTIFICATE OF DEATH/STATE OF GEORGIA

TYPE OR PRINT IN PERMANENT BLACK OR BLUE-BLACK INK

DECEASED

DECEDENT'S NAME (First, Middle, Last): Daniel McFarland Smith Jr.
IF DECEDENT IS FEMALE, ENTER MAIDEN LAST NAME:
SEX: Male
DATE OF DEATH (Mo., Day, Year): August 18, 2001
RACE (White, Black, Amer. Indian, etc.) (Specify): White
ORIGIN OF DECEDENT (Italian, Mex., French, English, etc.): American
DATE OF BIRTH (Mo., Day, Year): Oct 20, 1977
AGE-Last Birthday (Years): 23
COUNTY OF DEATH: Columbia
CITY, TOWN or LOCATION OF DEATH: Martinez 30907
HOSPITAL OR OTHER INSTITUTION NAME (If not in either, give street and No.): 3720 Columbia Dr.
IF HOSPITAL OR INST. (Indicate DOA, OP/EMER. Rm., Inpatient) (Specify): Residence
STATE AND COUNTY OF BIRTH (If not in USA, name Country): Ben Hill Co. GA
CITIZEN OF WHAT COUNTRY?: U.S.A.
MARRIED, NEVER MARRIED, WIDOWED, DIVORCED (Specify): Married
SPOUSE (If married or widowed, give spouse's name—If wife, give maiden name): Elizabeth Ashley Copeland
WAS DECEDENT EVER IN U.S. ARMED FORCES (Yes or No): No
SOCIAL SECURITY NUMBER: 257-29-7134
USUAL OCCUPATION (Give kind of work done during most of working life, even if retired): Carpenter
KIND OF INDUSTRY OR BUSINESS: Construction

Usual Residence Where Deceased Lived. If Death Occurred in Institution, See Handbook Regarding Completion of Residence Items.

RESIDENCE—STATE: Georgia
COUNTY: Columbia
CITY, TOWN or LOCATION: Martinez
STREET AND NUMBER: 3720 Columbia Dr. 30907
INSIDE CITY LIMITS (Yes or No): No

PARENTS

FATHER'S NAME: Daniel McFarland Smith
MOTHER'S MAIDEN NAME: Cynthia Anne Lee

INFORMANT

INFORMANT'S NAME: Elizabeth Ashley Smith
MAILING ADDRESS (Street, R.F.D. No., City or Town, State, Zip): 3720 Columbia Dr., Martinez, GA 30907
RELATIONSHIP: Wife

DISPOSITION

BURIAL, CREMATION, REMOVAL (Specify): Burial
DISPOSITION DATE (Mo., Day, Year): Aug 22, 2001
CEMETERY OR CREMATORY NAME: Bellevue Memorial Gardens
LOCATION (City or Town, State, Zip, County): Grovetown GA 30813 Columbia
FUNERAL DIRECTOR (Signature): Albert H. Jackson
FUN. DIR. LICENSE NO.: 3749
NAME AND ADDRESS OF FACILITY (Street, R.F.D. No., City or Town, State, Zip): Platt's Funeral Home, Inc. 337 N. Belair Road, Evans, GA 30809
EST. LICENSE NO.: 1357
EMBALMER (Signature): Cynthia J. Martin
EMBALMER LICENSE NO.: 3930

CAUSE OF DEATH

Conditions, If Any, Which Gave Rise To Immediate Cause Stating The Underlying Cause Last.

23. IMMEDIATE CAUSE: (Enter only one cause per line for A, B, and C)
PART I
A. Hemopericadium
Due to, or as a consequence of:
B. Hemo Throx
Due to, or as a consequence of:
C. Stab/incisid to chest
Approximate interval between onset and death

PART II 24. OTHER SIGNIFICANT CONDITIONS - conditions contributing to death but not related to cause given in Part IA. (If female, indicate if pregnant or birth occurred within 90 days of death.)
AUTOPSY (Yes or No): Yes
IF YES, WERE FINDINGS CONSIDERED IN DETERMINING CAUSE OF DEATH? (Yes or No): Yes

If Infant Death, Indicate Birth Certificate No. of Mate(s).

WAS OPERATION PERFORMED? (Yes or No): No
DATE OF OPERATION (Mo., Day, Year):
CONDITIONS FOR WHICH OPERATION WAS PERFORMED (Specify):
ACCIDENT, SUICIDE, HOMICIDE, UNDETERMINED (Specify): Homicide
DATE OF INJURY (Mo., Day, Year): August 18, 2001
DESCRIBE HOW INJURY OCCURRED: Fight
HOUR OF INJURY: approx 3:30 AM
INJURY AT WORK? (Yes or No): No
PLACE OF INJURY (Home, Farm, Street, Factory, Office, Etc.) (Specify): Street
LOCATION (Street, R.F.D. No., City or Town, State, Zip, County): Apple Cross Auto Martinez GA 30907 Columbia

CERTIFIER

To the best of my knowledge, death occurred at the time, date and place and due to the cause(s) stated. (Signature and Title)
On the basis of examination and/or investigation, in my opinion death occurred at the time, date and place and due to the cause(s) stated. (Signature and Title)
DATE SIGNED (Mo., Day, Year)
HOUR OF DEATH: 3:30 AM
PRONOUNCED DEAD: 3:30 PM

Form 3903

Top: Mack's death certificate. It was horrible getting this—to have to see the cause of death, time of death. "Homicide." My worst nightmare. Horrible.
Below: Mack's grave, Christmas 2002. Paige and I decorate on holidays.
I used to take her there when I was high on pills, just to sit. So unfair to her.

FBI agents after the surrender, March 12. I was terrified there would be a shoot-out and a lot of blood. I prayed like crazy. *Let him surrender!*

My apartment complex on the morning of March 12—
the place was crawling with cops, FBI agents, SWAT teams, you name it.

I couldn't believe it when I saw Brian Nichols coming down the hill without a fight. No gun in his hand. Head up. He had turned himself in. I just thanked God.

Brian Nichols in custody. I hope he knows that God is pleased he made the choice to surrender.

Left: Paige and me at my cousin Sarah's wedding last December. This was how I introduced Brian Nichols to my little girl. I would cry over this picture as I tried to gain his trust.

Four generations (above). "Mema," Mom, Paige, and me at our family reunion, June 2005. God blessed me with such a great, supportive family.

Aunt Kim and me, May 2005. Paige's end-of-the-year school program—the first one I attended at her new school. It was so special to me.

Left: Reconnecting with my little girl. Paige and me one recent Sunday after church. This is how we live every day now—side by side.

Me with my brother Christian at our family reunion, June 2005 (below). The first picture I've taken with him in six years. Just a sign of my isolation. Sad.

My sister Leah and me at her birthday party, June 2005. She wanted lots of photos taken. A happy time.

Judge-Sh
Heroine Award

The woman held hostage by a suspect in
of a judge in Atlanta was feted in the Georgia C
tol, and presented reward checks totaling $70,000.

Ashley Smith was lauded Thursday by a parade of state and local officials, who took turns presenting her with checks ranging from $5,000 to $25,000.

"My life is testimony that God can use us even in the midst of tragedy and that miracles do happen," Smith said.

The 26-year-old woman was held hostage for more than seven hours by Brian Nichols, who is suspected of killing four people, including Fulton County Superior Judge Rowland Barnes while escaping from a March 11 hearing regarding a rape charge.

Nichols encountered Smith about 2 a.m. March 12 and the woman said she talked to Nichols about her family and God. He allowed her to leave, ostensibly to visit her daughter, and she was able to call police. Nichols then surrendered without incident.

Smith had been praised for the calm she showed under the duress of the situation. She was rewarded financially with $25,000 from the U.S. Marshals Service, $20,000 from the FBI and four smaller checks.

UPI

March 24, 2005. With Georgia Governor Sonny Perdue at the Georgia capitol. I was humbled to be honored by him and the other officials. My life truly is a testimony that miracles do happen.

I remembered what my family had said about Mack shortly after we were married. Once they started getting to know him and seeing how smart he was, they called him "the brain surgeon of the remodeling field." Like the doctor of all doctors. The master of all. Mack could just walk into a room and picture something and say, "This is how it's gonna be." And it would turn out to be wonderful.

"We remodeled his parents' trailer," I told Brian. "I mean, from top to bottom—we ripped everything out of the whole entire trailer and put all new stuff back in. We ripped the flooring out, put in new appliances, redid the walls, painted everything, put in new windows. Mack retarred the roof. We just redid the whole thing.

"And then, when we had a house of our own, finally—I mean, we were renting it—but when we had that house, we painted all the rooms, and I painted the furniture for Paige's room. We put new floors in. It was like, Mack and I—we worked side by side."

I remembered what Mack used to say about me, bragging on me to his friends: "My wife can be one of the guys." That was a bond between us.

"Sometimes," I said, "when Mack was out on remodeling jobs, if he needed help, I'd go be his helper. I knew I didn't have to do it or anything—he just wanted me to stay home and be his wife—but I'm one of those people who needs to be doing something all the time or I'll go crazy."

I thought back to those days—dropping Paige off at her day school and showing up on Mack's job ready to work. He always had a specific way he liked things done. He would show me exactly what to do, and I'd be like, "Well, you're not showing me something I don't already know." But if I didn't do things Mack's way, then he just got mad. And I wasn't going to set him off. I knew all about that—I'd learned to run away from that boy's anger, not at it.

"I was probably a 'ride or die chick' for Mack," I told Brian. "You know that Tupac Shakur song that says 'ride or die'? Well, that used to be one of our songs. Mack would tell me, 'I need a ride or die chick.'

And I just did everything with him. Whatever he did, I was gonna do it. I had to be his wife. That's something I always did, was put him first. Even if it wasn't good, like with doing drugs together and stuff, I always put him first. I did what he did. That's just the kind of wife I was."

I was still working on the same cigarette and leaning against the bar, watching Brian. I liked standing there. I liked being able to see everything in the room and keep an eye on him. I felt safer that way, and I was too restless to sit right that minute.

"I mean, Mack and I were a little unsteady there for a while," I said. "Sometimes he would get mad—or I would set him off—and he'd just start beating and whaling on me." I was remembering the night Mack knocked me cold-slap-out in front of the club and left me there on the sidewalk. It was our last New Year's Eve together before he died, and we were fighting. Mack was drunk and angry. That's how it always was—until that very next morning when everything changed; when something clicked in Mack's mind and the fighting stopped for good.

"We didn't have an easy marriage," I went on. "But I loved Mack with all my heart, and I was going to do whatever had to be done to make it work for Paige. And really, both of us felt that way. Because of the way we grew up. I mean, I didn't have a daddy around. Mack had a really hard childhood and stuff. So we were gonna get it right, you know, get it right for her."

Brian didn't say a word. He uncrossed his legs. He looked at me. Wasn't he getting it about Paige now? Couldn't he see there was just no way I was leaving that child after everything I'd put into the marriage—and put into my life—to get it right?

"Mack and I were a team," I said to him. "We both had jobs that we would do. He would go make the money. Then he would bring me his check and I would pay all the bills. He could always count on me for organization and order like that.

"And I always cooked for him. Always. I cooked him breakfast. I made his lunch before he left every morning. And I had dinner ready the minute he walked in the door. I mean the *minute* he walked in. Sometimes Paige and I were there sitting at the table waiting for him to just sit down and start eating."

I could see Mack now, lying in the bed on Saturday mornings with Paige in his arms and the TV up on the dresser set to cartoons. That was how it was. Mack and I would have our Friday night out—we always had our Friday night. I would go meet his mom at the Bi-Lo halfway to their trailer in the country and drop Paige off with her. Then Mack and I would go out and party with our friends.

At about three or four in the morning we'd roll in. Then I'd sleep a few hours and drive out to the country to get Paige. I'd bring her home and stick her right in bed with Mack so they could watch cartoons. And I'd go to the kitchen and start breakfast—bacon, eggs, pancakes, whatever Mack wanted. That was my job. That was the way we started our weekends. And that was how it was supposed to be the morning after Mack died. I was just hours away from going to get Paige. Hours away from putting her in bed with him and cooking everybody Saturday breakfast.

I remembered thinking about all of that while Mack was stretched out in that parking lot hooked up to the paramedics' machine. "If he could just hold on a few more hours," I kept thinking as I watched the paramedics work. "Just a few more hours and he'll get to see Paige. I'm supposed to go get her and bring her home. We're supposed to have breakfast."

I looked over at Brian now, sitting there quietly on the couch. He was just letting me talk, one thing leading to the next—I was running my mouth like Mack used to say: "If you don't quit running your mouth, I'm gonna shut it for you."

I didn't say anything for a few seconds. I was remembering everything again. The evil in that parking lot. How wrong it all was. How it wasn't supposed to happen. Not then. Not when things were finally getting better with Mack and me. Didn't they understand? Mack was supposed to make it. For us. For Paige. "We're sorry," the EMT worker said. "He's gone." *Gone? But he didn't even get to say goodbye to her.*

Just then Brian stood up and stretched. "Is that the remote?" he asked, pointing. He was looking at the TV sitting on top of the tall chest of drawers on the wall just opposite him. The remote was sitting beside it.

"Uh, yeah," I said, putting out my cigarette. "Yeah, but it doesn't work. You have to turn it on at the set. But, sure. Go ahead. Turn on the TV if you want."

18 the news

I stood at the bar by the kitchen watching Brian. He was standing right in front of the TV flipping the channels. He looked very alert, as if searching for something specific. Then I heard it. His name. On the TV. Just like I had heard it before I left my house for cigarettes, although I wasn't really paying much attention then. "Brian Nichols," the announcer said. *Brian Nichols.*

Brian turned up the volume and went back to where he was sitting on the couch. He had set the TV on channel 33, CNN. I couldn't believe what I was seeing. There he was, coming out of the courthouse it looked like, in that black suit, going down some stairs. He was loose. Running around like that. And no one was catching him. I couldn't believe it.

Then they started talking about the people he had killed at the courthouse. Showing photographs. I just stood there frozen. *Oh, God, help me. This is—This is—Lord, what am I in right here? This is* so *not good.*

I turned and glanced at Brian. He looked as scared as I felt right then. *Okay, I'm not going to let him see me scared. I'm just going to watch this TV and focus on it and stay calm.*

I knew I had to hold it together. I couldn't let Brian start thinking I was against him—that I saw him as some terrible person like they were saying on the news. He wouldn't trust me then. He wouldn't let me go. And so far I thought I'd done a pretty good job of not making him feel like a criminal. I mean, he had tied me up. And he had the guns and everything. But basically I had tried to treat him like a normal person, kind of like one of my friends — telling him about my life; reading to him out of my book. And I thought it was working. I thought I was gaining his trust.

Thinking back over the hours, I couldn't believe I'd even survived this long. *How long have we been in here? How long have I been doing this?* I guessed it was going on 5:00 a.m., and I was starting to feel exhausted. It just had to be God keeping me from totally freaking out. "Ashley," I could imagine God saying, "you can't lose it now. Just be you. You'll be all right if you just be yourself." Somehow I'd kept it together till now. Whatever time it was, I knew there had to be several hours left until 9:30. So I had to keep going. I had to stay focused. And I kept my eyes on the TV.

The news flashed back to that footage of Brian Nichols in the black suit escaping out of what I guessed was the courthouse. I could feel my heart beating faster in my chest. *How is this guy sitting in my apartment right now? Why my apartment? This is crazy.* I tried to focus on the whole miracle thing again and God having a purpose. Maybe that would give him some hope. And give me some hope.

So I said, "Look, Brian. What's the deal here? I mean, how did you get here? How did you make it?"

Honestly, I just didn't understand. The chances of him (a) making it out of that courthouse and (b) getting to my apartment were just — well, it was just incredible. I mean, how did he get out of there with all those police officers around? They didn't shoot at him or anything. They didn't even see him. Surely when all the commotion started inside the building, someone told the cops outside. Why didn't anybody see him when he ran out?

"So you came down those steps and no one saw you?" I asked him. "How could no one see you? I mean, you could've been shot and killed right there. All those people were around. And you didn't even get hurt and now you're sitting here in my apartment?" I took out another cigarette and lit it, standing up straight next to the bar to face him. I could see the TV screen in the mirror propped on the back of the sofa just above his head.

"Dude, you totally escaped from jail and that's not a freakin' miracle to you? I mean, if you don't think it's a total miracle that you're sitting here alive right now, then I don't know what to tell you." I kind of studied him for a minute. *What's he thinking, looking at all this stuff?*

Brian was just leaning back, staring at the TV screen. His eyes were wide open. His mouth was hanging open a little. He sat there looking scared. Like a little boy. Like he was in shock maybe. I couldn't even imagine. "Yeah," he said then, not moving. "Yeah, I guess it was God or something." He was talking so low I could barely hear him over the TV.

I wanted to get off my feet, so, picking up the ashtray, I walked around the coffee table to the other side of the couch, the far right corner, and sat down. Then I reached back and pulled up my jeans to keep my underwear from showing, and I kind of sat with my lower back pressed into the leather in the corner. I really wanted to just change clothes, or at least put on my sweater; but I was afraid I would draw attention to myself that way. My sweater was probably still in a heap by the front door. And I didn't want him walking in on me or anything if I tried to go and change.

But Brian wasn't paying attention to me right then. He was sitting forward on the couch now, with his elbows on his knees, staring a hole through that TV screen.

I heard the news anchor say something about a car they had found—something about a car Brian Nichols had ditched somewhere.

"Yeah," Brian said, still looking at the TV. "Yeah, because I took MARTA after that."

To me this was just getting more amazing by the second. I didn't know anything about these details. "Okay," I said to him. "So you got out of the courthouse, then you got on a MARTA train? Without anyone catching you? And you made it out here to Duluth to an apartment I just moved into two days ago? What are the chances, dude? You've got to see God's hand in this."

I couldn't get past it—the whole thing. *I just know this is God right here. It has to be.* But then what did it mean? So God brought the guy to my apartment. Okay. Why? Maybe part of it was to see what I would do with those drugs. Maybe it was something else. I didn't know. *I guess I'm just hanging onto you, God, and waiting. That's all I know to do. I mean, this is way bigger than me. Way bigger.* I figured all I could do was keep doing what I was doing—try to get through to this guy so he would stop running and hurting people, try to gain his trust, and wait it out till 9:30.

I looked over at the TV and heard the anchor say something about Brian Nichols and a deputy. He had shot a deputy, a woman, the anchor said.

Right then Brian jumped up and started yelling at the screen. "I didn't shoot that lady! I hit her over the head!" He was looking at the TV like he was fed up, amazed, angry—something. Then he turned to me again with his eyes wide open. "I hope she lives," he said. I saw that same fear in his eyes. That same look of almost panic.

"Please let her live," he said now, looking up at the ceiling and raising his hands. "I'm sorry! Please forgive me." *He's asking God to forgive him. He's doing it. This means something. I know this is big—for both of us.*

At that moment I slid onto the floor, got on my knees, and faced the sofa. *Thank you, God. Just thank you for getting me this far.*

Now Brian was sitting down again—leaning back on the couch and watching the TV. He seemed really mellow all of a sudden. Really quiet. Looking at him, I didn't know what to feel. I felt bad for him—just seeing the remorse, seeing how scared he was. But then at the same time, I stepped back from him and was like, "Okay. This guy's done wrong. He took people's lives. He has to pay."

For a minute or two, I just zoned out on the couch and smoked my cigarette. My pocketbook was still sitting on the coffee table next to a chunky purple candle. Just to my left was the tan recliner that belonged to the guy from Augusta; and next to that, the door to the front porch. My keys were sitting out on Paige's toy box. In the partially lit room, the TV was making shadows on the walls, and out of the corner of my eye I saw Brian shift a little where he was sitting.

"I wonder what my family's thinking right now," he said, still staring at the TV. "My mother—she's probably watching this in Africa right now, going, 'What's he doing? That's not my son.'"

I thought: "All right. He's feeling alone. Totally alone. Like nobody can relate to him. So that means *I've* got to keep relating to him. I've got to keep talking straight to him like he's a regular person with responsibilities, so he doesn't flip out and want to go hurt himself or something."

"I just—" he said, sitting up over his knees on the edge of the sofa and watching the screen, "I just can't believe that's me up there—on that TV."

Okay. Here I go. Talking straight now. Talking to him like he's a man. "Well, yeah," I said, reaching over to the coffee table to ash my cigarette in the ashtray. "It is you. It's you up there, Brian, and you're gonna have to pay for what you did. You know that."

I wasn't feeling scared of him really—scared that he would hurt me for saying what I said. He hadn't touched the guns since doing the drugs. They were still all spread out on the bathroom counter. And he was so calm—just shocked maybe—that, I don't know, I just didn't feel he wanted to hurt anybody else. At least not right then.

So I kept going. "You know, you have to take responsibility for your actions here. That's what you have to do. I've had to take responsibility for my actions. I've made bad decisions, and I've had to face those. And now I'm learning to correct the bad decisions with good decisions."

I was thinking about how much I hated that ride out to recovery with my mom. She had told me she wasn't going to make me go. I'd been sleeping on her couch in Atlanta for ten days—sleeping eighteen hours a day trying to dry out. I didn't need any help, I told her. I could dry out and get it together just fine by myself. I'd already gone without drugs for ten days.

Really, though, I was scared to death. John had just gotten busted in Augusta, and Aunt Kim would no longer let me see Paige. I had left town for Atlanta because I didn't know what else to do. Lying on my mom's couch all those days, I kept remembering the lights flashing on those police cars the night of the bust as I sat in John's car in front of that house. The cops were rounding up people, and they said to me, "We know you're pregnant. We know you're going to rehab. Just get out of here. Just go."

I was pregnant, all right. And I was doing ice like nuts then. I couldn't even stop for my baby. Couldn't even come close to stopping. I might have tried for a couple of days, but I didn't try all that hard—I just went back to hot railing every several hours. And I knew I was really in trouble, really in deep with those drugs, because I wasn't just destroying myself now. I was destroying my baby. All the time I would ask myself, "You can't even stop for a life God's given you, Ashley?" And the answer was no. I was so weak. Every time, the answer was no.

After the bust and those first few days of drying out in Atlanta, I learned that I had lost the baby; I miscarried at five weeks. And I was just wrecked over it. I knew it was my fault. Nothing but my own stupid, selfish, pathetic drug use had brought on that miscarriage. Facing that fact was just devastating. I mean, I couldn't even stop for a child. Well, I was stopping now. I was scared to death. I was lying on my mom's couch, and I was just going to sleep there as long as it took.

Finally, my mom said, "Look, Ashley, you've gotta go somewhere." I was totally ticked off at her for saying that. Couldn't she see I was doing this myself? I just wanted everybody to leave me alone and let me dry out.

But then she said, "You know, Aunt Kim's never going to give Paige back if you don't finish recovery." So I had to think. I really had to think. Think about my choices. Think about the future. I had tried recovery programs twice already and failed to finish. Did I want Paige back or not? Did I want to be fit to be her mom? I had to think about those questions and be honest with myself. In the end I said, "Okay, fine. I failed those other times. I've gotta go to recovery. I have to finish. Fine."

Brian was still staring at the TV, and I started talking again. *God, just get him to listen to me here.*

"It's like what I learned in recovery," I told him now, taking a long drag on my cigarette. "I had to face my failures and, you know, the mistakes I'd made and just quit hiding from them. Quit running. Quit wallowing in self-pity. I mean, nobody made me do those drugs up my nose. Nobody forced me. That was my decision. And I had to quit blaming other people. Quit blaming Mack for not listening to me. Just quit blaming everybody and own up. You know, take responsibility."

Is he hearing me? I couldn't tell. Maybe he was listening. Maybe he wasn't. But I was going to keep on until I got through to this guy. I didn't care if he wanted me to shut up or go crawl under a rock somewhere. This right here, this stuff I was telling him—I knew this was what he needed to hear. I knew what he needed to do. And I was starting to feel that it was my job to talk to him until he saw it. To just run my mouth, like Mack said, until he got it and really knew in his heart what to do and could make the right decision.

"I've had to correct my bad decisions with good decisions," I said again, turning to face him. "That's what I'm doing here trying to build a life for Paige. And that's what you've got to do now, Brian. You've got to turn yourself in and pay for what you did. That's a good decision. That's the right thing to do. That's what a real man would do. A real man would face up to his actions and step up and take responsibility."

He didn't say anything. He didn't move. The TV was blaring, and I kept hearing his name while I was talking. "Brian Nichols." I tried to ignore it and keep on.

"You know one thing that helps me sometimes is this verse—it's on my screensaver. Philippians 4:13, 'I can do all things through Christ who strengthens me.' When I think about Paige and being a mother, it's like I get scared to death of just failing and not making it. And I say that verse to myself, you know, to keep going. So maybe it might help you too."

No response. Just the TV and the news anchor and the whole city wondering where Brian Nichols could be right now. *Hello! He's sitting on my couch watching you guys. In the apartment I just moved into. In the back section of this random apartment complex in Duluth. He's not in Alabama. Not even close.* I smoked and tried to tune it all out for a minute.

I was remembering being sent to the fence line at recovery. I'd broken the rules and said a few cuss words, and Miss Kate just let me have it. "You can go learn some humility," she said. She was all about humility. "You go work over there by yourself, and you pull weeds." I was taken off the pine forest crew and sent to the fence, where there were tons of weeds growing.

"This is so stupid," I thought, yanking up the weeds. "I'm pulling weeds—how much humility is this? This isn't bringing me any humility." I was getting madder and madder, but I couldn't leave that fence line. That whole "I don't care about anything" attitude from the drugs wasn't going to work here. If I got up from that fence, they would've sent me home in a heartbeat. And then I would've failed again. And I couldn't do that. Because of Paige. I had to stay there with those weeds and get my humility and keep going so I could make it for her.

Suddenly, looking at Brian now, I thought, "I'm gonna ask him this question. Maybe if I ask it, he'll start talking to me about what he did instead of sitting there looking like he could just blow his own head off. Maybe if he talks, he can start facing it and looking at his options and realize he's got to stop now. Stop and own up."

I reached over and put out my cigarette in the ashtray. Then I put my hands in my lap and looked over at him. He was still leaning back. Still looking really low key. Really down. *Maybe I shouldn't do this. It might make him worse.* But then I thought, "Yes. I'm asking, because he seems emotional right here. Like he's feeling it. And I've got to get him to face his choices while he's at least feeling something." *I'm going for it.*

"So," I said, taking a deep breath. "Why'd you do it?"

19 you're not dead

Brian didn't say anything. He didn't move. He had laid his head back on the sofa, and he looked as if he was about to pass out.

I looked past him into the dining room. I didn't know what to do with that mattress and box springs leaning against the wall. I wanted my mom to take them, but she didn't have room.

"I deserve a bullet in the back," he said suddenly, kind of mumbling it. His eyes were half-closed. He was still looking at the TV, or at least looking in that direction. But he really was just in this terrible funk. *I've got to talk him into another frame of mind here, God. I don't want this guy blowing his brains out in that bathroom back there. I don't think I could handle that.*

I sat up Indian-style on the couch and turned toward him. "Look," I said. "Nobody deserves to die. But you do have to pay for what you did. Everybody has to pay for the mistakes they've made and the wrongs they've done. I'm paying for mine like I told you. I'm not able to raise Paige right now. And that's just the way things are. We have to take responsibility for our actions."

I was thinking again about all of the back and forth with God over the drugs these last months—calling that guy and yet praying for him not to be there. I mean, why couldn't I just have decided not to pick up the phone in the first place? Why did I keep making that mistake? I remembered saying to God, "Lord, I'm tired of making the same mistake. Please, please, please let me learn from the mistake, and before I make that same mistake again, let me step back and look at it and go, 'Ashley, you're about to make the same mistake.' Let me think about it like they said in recovery, instead of just going ahead and acting and making that same old mistake."

Looking at Brian all sprawled back on the sofa, I knew I was going to have to keep talking about paying for my mistakes and accepting responsibility and all of that stuff until I got through to him. He had to snap out of this haze and start thinking forward about the decisions he had in front of him. *Let's just face what's happened here, buddy, deal with it, and move forward to what you're going to do now.* I didn't want him having a breakdown. What could I say right now to help this guy get it together and see what he had to do and find some hope?

"Okay," I thought, "maybe I should try asking that question again." If I could just get him to engage with me, then maybe I could get somewhere. *God, help me.*

"Why'd you do it?" I asked him again.

He turned his head in my direction. Then he said, "I didn't belong in there. I didn't belong in there, and I had to do whatever it took to get out."

Right then I thought maybe I was starting to understand a little bit of what had happened to him at that courthouse. I was thinking about what he had said earlier in the bathroom. *She falsely accused me of rape. She went out with one of our ministers.* Maybe his heart was just broken. Maybe he *was* falsely accused.

And his child had just been born—I mean, his son was born, and there he was in jail. Maybe he just exploded with frustration and anger. Maybe he just wanted out so badly he went crazy, totally flipped, and started shooting. I could understand how that could happen to somebody.

I was seeing Mack in that apartment complex again the night he died. He had been fighting those guys for what seemed like hours. Now he was going back for more, and he was carrying the pole he always kept in the back of his truck—it was a pole made for a closet; the kind you were supposed to hang clothes on.

"No, honey!" I called out to Mack. "You're done here! You've had your say!" This had been going on way too long. "Honey, let's go now! You're done!" But Mack was really angry—something inside of him had just exploded and taken over. He wasn't listening to me. He wouldn't listen. He didn't hear a word I said. "Okay!" he was yelling, carrying that pole. "Who wants some now?"

I looked over at Brian. His head was still back. His face looked washed out. His hands were on his knees. The khakis were riding up his calves. He just didn't look good. Didn't look good at all. *This has got to end now. It has to end. He can't go on like this. It's done. It has to be done.*

"You're done," I had told Mack that night. But he wouldn't listen. *Why couldn't he just listen to me for once?*

Sitting across from Brian on the couch now, I was starting to feel bolder—I felt that God was making me bolder. *I don't want to die. I don't want anybody else to die. And I don't want this guy to die, either. He's done enough. He's got to know that. I've just got to make him know that.*

Right then I started to realize I was going to have to keep working until I didn't have anything left. I was going to have to convince this guy to turn himself in so nobody else got hurt. That was what God wanted me to do. I saw it now. I really saw it. That was why I was here on my couch in this apartment in Duluth with Brian Nichols. That was why Brian had picked this apartment complex. That was why he had pulled up right when I was going out for cigarettes. This was my purpose right here—to help him stop hurting people. I was seeing it. This was my destiny. I just had to keep talking and do everything I could to get Brian to see what God wanted him to do. *Just make me bold, God. Keep giving me confidence. Help me.*

"You know," I said, "if you don't stop and turn yourself in now, lots more people are going to get hurt."

He had come into my apartment saying he didn't want to hurt anybody else, and right now he actually looked like he didn't want to do it anymore. So I was going to keep bringing that up, keep going back to what he originally said. Just elaborate on his own desire and let him see what the consequences would be if he didn't stop running.

"Nobody else needs to get hurt, dude," I said again. "And if you don't turn yourself in, somebody else *will* get hurt. You'll keep going and you'll kill more people and you'll probably die too." I knew that if he kept running, he would need money, and I could just picture him robbing the bank like he said or holding somebody up and then something really, really bad going down.

"I don't want that," he said. *Thank you. He's starting to think now. Think about his choices. He's hearing me.* I just kept on with it. Kept saying what I wanted him to do.

"Okay, so you've got to turn yourself in and pay for it. You don't want it to get worse. Either you'll kill more people or somebody's going to kill you."

He turned his head toward me again. Then he paused for a few seconds. "Look at me," he said. "Look at my eyes. I'm already dead."

For a minute I felt my face flush. This was heavy. He was in a total pit of despair. What if I couldn't do it? What if I couldn't convince him to turn himself in? I mean, what he ultimately decided to do was his choice. I couldn't *make* him listen to me. I couldn't *make* him turn himself in. Mack didn't listen. That was his choice. He didn't listen—and he died. *What if this guy keeps going, God? What if he doesn't let me leave? You've got to work with me. I can't do it alone. I just can't do it alone.*

Brian went back to watching TV, and I leaned back into the corner of the sofa. *He already feels dead. He has no hope.* I knew what that felt like. My life was turning around now, and I was on my way back up; but I had been there at the bottom with no hope. Feeling dead in my heart, dead in my spirit, just dead.

I was remembering that terrible year of hot railing—going to that place we called the crack house and making drug runs to Atlanta with John. I was so wigged out, so crazy and paranoid, that I thought I literally was a ghost walking around. I thought I was dead and nobody could see me. When I would call my mom and she wouldn't answer her phone, I would think, "She's not picking up because it's not even ringing because I'm a freakin' ghost and this isn't even real what I'm doing here trying to make this call." I was probably having a nervous breakdown, just completely losing my mind.

I knew what it was like to feel dead, gone, off the planet, totally hopeless; and I didn't want Brian to feel that way. He needed hope for his life. I mean, he was going to prison. He couldn't really raise his child. I knew how that felt. But there still had to be hope. If there wasn't hope, then what reason would he have to stop running and hurting people? What reason would he have not to hurt himself? I sat up now and looked hard at him.

"No," I said. "You are not dead. You're alive. You're alive, and you're sitting right here in front of me. If you want to die, you can. It's your choice. But you're not dead now."

He kept staring at the TV. After a few seconds he said in that low, flat tone of voice, "I'm gonna fry. I'm really gonna fry." Then he turned to me and said, "You know, I'd rather you go in there and get those guns and shoot me yourself. I'd rather you shoot me than them."

This was not good. I shook my head at him. "No way, dude," I said. "I'm not doing that. I'm not gonna be your assassinator. I'm not breaking that commandment. And I don't want anyone else to die—not even you." *God, don't let him get some crazy idea that he can make me do that. Just take that out of his mind right now. You know I'm not doing that. And I'm walking out of here in the morning.*

"No," I went on, "you've got to turn yourself in and pay for this. You've got a son now. And it's gonna take more of a man to turn yourself in than it is not to turn yourself in and kill me or hurt more people or hurt yourself. You've got to see that now. You've gotta be a man. Don't you want to make it for your son?"

He didn't say anything. And I didn't like the way this was going. I didn't like what I was seeing on his face. I didn't like him watching that TV.

"Will you turn that off, please?" I said suddenly, standing up and walking over to the kitchen. "I don't want to hear that."

I was seeing pain in his eyes, and I just didn't want him watching that stuff anymore, watching all those people talk about what he had done and what a terrible person he was. It wasn't good for him to be hearing those things. He had to keep believing that he had a reason to live, a reason to stop and do the right thing. He was already facing the truth of what he'd done a little bit, and I figured that little bit was enough. He didn't need to fall apart and go back to the bathroom where those guns were.

"Would you mind turning off the TV?" I asked again. Now I was standing at the kitchen sink, right behind the bar, and looking at him over the row of picture frames. He was still in that same position, still lying back on the sofa. I could see the news playing in that mirror above his head, and I didn't know if he could even hear me. Then he stood up slowly and started walking toward the TV.

20 tools and a badge

"Are you hungry?" I asked him now.

I was standing in the kitchen on the other side of the bar. We had been going at this for a long time. He was hungry earlier, so I knew he had to be hungry now. And I actually thought I could eat too. I needed something to keep going—I knew that much.

"Yeah," he said, turning to face me where he stood in front of the TV. "That sounds good."

I walked over to the stove and opened the same cabinet of dry foods I had showed him earlier. I thought I would make pancakes. That would be easy. I figured morning would be here soon enough, so I might as well make breakfast.

Then he asked, "Do you have a computer?"

"Yes," I said, still facing the cabinet. "It's in my bedroom, but it's not hooked up yet."

He didn't say anything. I figured he wanted to get on the Internet, and I was just glad that wasn't an option for him. He needed to quit thinking about all of that stuff right now.

Behind me, I could hear him walking around—in the hallway and then the living room. Then I heard the front door open and close. A minute later it opened again, and when I turned around to look, I saw him bringing in a twelve-pack of Coors Light with some of the cans missing. He came around the bar to the fridge and stuck the beer in there. He was wearing my brown leather clogs.

"You want a beer?" he asked, grabbing one.

"No thanks." I just wasn't drinking beer with this guy.

Then he said, "I've gotta make a move." *A move? I don't like the sound of that.*

He walked out of the kitchen now, and I went back to getting the ingredients out for breakfast. The way the kitchen was set up, if you turned your back to the sink and the living room, the stove was to your left, the microwave was on the counter in front of you, the fridge was to the far right, and in between was counter space. I was basically moving around, trying to think about where I had put things when I unpacked.

I took the box of pancake mix and some cooking oil down from the cabinet. I got the big pan out from underneath the stove. I took some eggs out of the refrigerator. I went to the utensil drawer for a spatula, whisk, and wooden spoon. If I needed it, the canister of sugar was already out on the counter. Mack and I had gotten a set of three canisters—white with big fruits on them—as a wedding gift, but one canister broke during a move. The two I had left were just to the right of the microwave next to my coffeepot.

I wasn't really paying much attention to Brian at this point. I had been on guard for so long, maybe I was just tired—and glad to have something to do. I could hear him moving around and then going in and out of the front door. For whatever reason, it never occurred to me to just go over there and lock him out. I mean, I had the guns inside with me. I could've done it. But I just wasn't thinking like that. I was focused on waiting until 9:30 so that he would let me leave, and nobody would have to get hurt. That's where my mind was.

At some point, though, I turned and glanced over the bar, and I saw Brian come into the apartment carrying something. He walked in and set whatever it was down in front of that low, whitewashed bench I had covered. Then he turned around and walked out again. A minute or two later he was back. From where I was standing in the kitchen, I could see his shoulders and head as he walked into the living room. Then I saw his head duck behind the bar again as he set something else down.

When he turned to go back out, I looked over the picture frames sitting on the bar and saw what he was bringing in—tools. I knew tools. Mack had a whole shed full of tools, and I knew which tools were which. I knew what a circular saw looked like. I knew what a miter saw looked like. I knew what a drill looked like. I could recognize the different boxes they were stored in. Looking at the lineup in front of the bar, I knew those were some pretty expensive tools right there.

Brian was coming back in now with another load, and as he set it down, I said, "What are you doing with all this?"

"These are yours now," he said, gesturing at the floor. He was talking to me across the bar. "I've gotta make a move, and you can have these. Maybe you can start your own business or something and do what you've always dreamed of."

What? He wants to help me fulfill my dreams? I was maybe touched that he'd actually listened to what I said about fixing stuff and decorating and all that, but something was not right here. Not right at all. And I still didn't know what he meant by "make a move."

"Dude, these are some really nice tools. Where'd you get these from?"

"From this guy, this agent," he said. *Agent? Like CIA agent?*

Now he looked down at the floor as he talked. "I didn't—I didn't want to kill him. All I needed was his truck, you know, and like I begged him—begged him—to listen to me and just cooperate and do what I told him. But he wouldn't. He just kept fighting me back, so I had to kill him."

Whoa! Okay. I didn't know about this. There's someone else. He's killed someone else. Someone who wasn't at the courthouse. Oh, God, help me here. Help me not to panic. Just keep me focused on what we're doing. I'm making breakfast. We're doing good. He's going to let me leave. He's going to stop and turn himself in. I was trying to get some air and not let him see me shake or anything. I was glad the sink and the bar were between us. *God, just help.*

Then I saw that Brian was holding a wallet in his hand. "I got his wallet," he said lifting the wallet up. "He was an agent. Yeah, here's his badge." Now he walked around the bar to the kitchen and stood in front of me, flipping the wallet open. The badge was inside. "This is him right here."

I focused on the badge, trying to keep my head together. There were all kinds of credit cards in the wallet that Brian could've already started using. Then I looked down at the agent's driver's license. I looked at his photograph. He was a young guy. Maybe forty years old. He was probably a husband and a father. I thought about Mack right then. I thought about what Paige had lost. What I had lost. What we had been through. And I could feel my adrenaline kick in. I could feel my heart racing. I could feel rage coming up. Like I wanted to scream.

"Look at this guy," I told Brian now, pointing at that wallet. "Look at him. He's probably forty. Do you know what that means? It means you took away somebody's husband. And probably somebody's father. Do you realize that? Do you know what that feels like? Can you imagine it?"

He just stood there, holding the wallet open. I could see that his thumb was bleeding, probably from carrying the tools. I kept going. And I wasn't holding back.

"Well, let me explain it to you," I started. "Let me tell you about Paige and what she lost."

I was thinking about what Paige had been telling Aunt Kim lately—how other kids at her school had their daddies and why didn't she have hers? And why couldn't she be with her mommy, either? I was just sick over it. Sick.

"You know," I said, "Paige will never, ever have her father. He's gone. He's not coming back. She will never get to spend time with the man who loved her most—her daddy. Because someone took that away from her. Just ripped him out of her life before she could even really know him. She was just two. Two years old.

"I mean, Mack wasn't always around because he worked so much, but he loved Paige to death. He gave her anything she wanted. He provided for us. He was an incredible provider. It didn't matter if he was worn out from working—he was going to provide for us and give us whatever he thought we needed. That was a huge thing to him. We were going to have the best whether we wanted it or not, because he was going to give it to us."

I was remembering Mack on his lunch breaks—how he would sneak back to the house to lie on the sofa with Paige. "Honey," I said, "I'm not going to keep making your lunch every day if you're just coming back home." He would be stretched out on our striped sofa with Paige in his arms. Just holding her.

"Mack loved Paige," I said to Brian now, taking a step back from him. "He would lie on the couch with her and let her draw all over him after a long day at work. One time he said to me, 'You don't bathe her right.' 'What?' I said. 'I look after this child every day while you're gone and you can bet I get every crevice in her body.' 'No,' he said. 'You don't bathe her right. I'm gonna show you how to bathe her.' And he did. I just let him do his thing, and he bathed her right there, showing me how he thought it should be done." *Is this guy hearing me? He's got to feel this.*

"Mack had a huge heart," I said. "He had a huge, generous heart, and Paige will never get to know it now. She'll never feel his love. She'll never know her daddy's heart. Never have his arms around her. And I feel so sorry for her. I feel sorry for her because it's not fair. It's not fair somebody took her daddy away. Somebody killed him. Do you hear me? He's gone. Her daddy's gone. And she didn't even get the chance to say goodbye."

For a minute I was back in that parking lot again. With those paramedics. And Mack hooked up to that machine. "Give more air. Breathe. Give more air. Breathe." His body was so toned and tan from all of the hard work outside. He was stocky and powerful. He always had huge amounts of energy. But he was lying there now. His eyes were closed. He wasn't moving. "Give him more air!" I yelled. "Breathe!"

"Not now, baby," I was thinking. "Not now. Not when we're finally getting it right. This isn't supposed to be happening now."

As I looked at Mack lying there lifeless next to that machine, I thought back to the morning when everything changed for us. That morning when something inside of Mack snapped, and he got clear on how he wanted to live. It was New Year's Day, our last New Year's together. Mack had stormed into the house yelling at the top of his lungs: "We're getting a divorce!" I was standing in the living room holding Paige. Mack's face was all cut up and bruised. The night before he had knocked me unconscious in front of that club and left me there on the sidewalk. Some men had gone after him—he said it was the police—and now he was blaming me. "They beat the crap out of me because of you," he screamed. "And we're getting a divorce!"

Looking at his swollen face, I smiled kind of sarcastically. My head was still pounding from the blow the night before. "Divorce?" I said. "Um, no we're not, honey. We're not getting a divorce." I lifted Paige up. "Look! Do you see her? Remember? We're staying together for her."

Mack was holding a cup in his hand, and in one quick motion he turned and whipped that cup right at me. Whatever was in it splattered all over Paige and me and the wall behind us. I stood there looking at Mack, not knowing what to say or do. And then I saw his expression change. He stopped where he was. "Wait a minute," he said, whispering. "What am I doing? You're my wife. She's my child." He sat down on the sofa. "I'm sorry," he said, putting his bruised face in his hands. "I'm so sorry."

He never laid a hand on me after that. Our marriage started to get better, and Mack began to really love me—not just because I was his wife, but for who I was. He spent more time at home. It started to feel like we were a family. I could see my prayers being answered. And then he was taken away. Gone, they said. "He's gone."

"Do you know what it did to me losing my husband?" I said to Brian now. He was holding the wallet at his side, looking down at the floor. "I already told you what it did to me. I lost it, man. I went completely down. I was scared to death. I felt completely alone in this world. How was I ever going to take care of Paige and provide for her? I was totally devastated. I didn't want to feel anything ever again. I just wanted to pretend it wasn't happening.

"I was taking all those pain pills and Xanaxes and going out and getting high every time I could. Just leaving Paige whenever I had the chance. I mean, I checked out on her. I didn't give her any attention. I took those pills in front of her. I drove her around like that. I mean, I could've killed her. Could've killed us both and other people too. Are you hearing me?

"I would drive her to the cemetery all messed up on pills and make her sit there at her daddy's grave playing with these little wind chimes while I cried and talked to Mack for hours. How do you think that made her feel? To have to see her mommy like that? And then I started with the ice and the paranoia. And sending her to live at Aunt Kim's. And my car accident. And moving away to Atlanta. Do you know how many times Paige has asked me, 'Mommy, when's your scar from the accident gonna get better so I can come live with you?' And here I've been still using those drugs and getting messed up, still playing with that stuff, trying to convince myself I can do it and still be a good mom.

"I mean, Brian—how do you think Paige feels? What do you think she must feel about her mommy now? It's shameful what I've put her through. Don't you get it?" I was pointing at the wallet in his hand. "Don't you see? That man's family is going to have to survive what you've just put *them* through. You ripped that man away just like those people took Mack. You did that. And this family has to survive it."

I took another step back now. I was almost afraid to look Brian in the eye after what I had just said. But he had to hear it. It was time for him to suck it up and deal. He had to face it head-on. He had to see what he had really, really done. He had to know he was going to have to pay for this.

Clearing his throat, Brian closed the wallet and set it down on the end of the bar next to Paige's picture in that big silver frame. I was looking down at the navy rug I'd put down in this kitchen yesterday. It covered the entire floor. Then I remembered his bleeding thumb.

"Look, man," I said, reaching out my hand. "Your finger's bleeding. Let me—just, come here and let me put something on it."

21 a certificate

I stepped over to the sink and turned on the water. "Here," I said again, reaching for his hand, "let me put a Band-Aid on it and let's clean it off."

He stretched out his hand, and I took it, looking at the cut. It was a small cut on his thumb right by his nail. "Let's put it under the water," I said, pulling him forward so I could stick his thumb under the faucet. "Keep it right there."

Then I turned to the cabinet above the microwave and took down my small first-aid basket. I grabbed the bottle of peroxide and went back to the sink.

"Okay," I said, opening the bottle, "take your thumb out of the water and hold it right here." He did what I said, and I poured the peroxide over his cut. "Now wait." I stepped over to the counter and pulled a paper towel off the roll. Then I went back and blotted his thumb dry so the Band-Aid would stick.

"Step over here now." I reached into my first-aid basket, got out the box of Band-Aids, and opened it. "Stick out your thumb." I peeled the wrapper off a Band-Aid and wrapped it around his thumb, covering his nail. "Okay," I told him, "that should do it."

He pulled his hand back and looked at the job I'd done. "Thanks," he said.

"Sure."

To me, Brian looked very calm standing there examining his thumb. I was guessing everything I had just said to him was sinking in now. And I felt calm too. Just a strange peace. It was like the presence of the Lord was here in the apartment—just like when I did my devotions in the mornings. Just a peace filling the whole place. Filling my whole heart. I couldn't understand it.

I remembered that dark presence of evil I felt in the parking lot the night Mack died—and even after that night. When I tried to go back to the apartment complex later and leave a candle for Mack, I felt it then too. I couldn't even drive up to the spot where he died to put the candle down. I just got out of the car, left the candle on a curb, and got out of there. Darkness. Evil. Like nothing that happened there that night was of God. They took Mack away in the ambulance and wouldn't let me be with him. It was all wrong. Just wrong.

But standing here in my kitchen right now with Brian Nichols, I felt the complete opposite. Like there was this presence of God all around me. God was with me. I knew that now. I could feel it. God had a purpose here. My husband was gone—he was dead. I was still here for some reason. Paige needed me. God had something for me to do, and I was doing it. I was telling Brian what he needed to hear, trying to help him quit hurting people and turn himself in. Somehow I was able to stay focused and do the next thing. I just knew God was doing his will right here. I really knew it.

Suddenly, I had an idea. "I'll be right back," I told Brian.

I walked across the living room to the hallway and turned into my bedroom. *Okay, God, help me put my hands on that piece of paper fast.*

Stepping into my closet, I went straight to my plastic file drawers on the left-hand side. Sitting on top of them was the box of file folders that wouldn't fit in those drawers. All of my files were labeled, and I knew exactly what this one folder looked like. *Here it is.* Opening it up, I started flipping through papers. My car accident report. Paige's custody papers. My release letter from recovery. My letter to the judge about my progress. A copy of my wedding invitation. Those laminated articles about Mack's death. Then: *Here it is. Found it. Good.*

I pulled out the sheet of paper, stuck the folder in the box, and walked back into the living room. Brian was standing beside the bar, next to that lineup of expensive tools he had taken from the agent.

"Look," I said, walking toward him, holding out the piece of paper. "Look at this. This is what that man's wife and kids are going to have to look at. This is what they get to go through. I did, and they will too. Look."

Brian reached out and took the paper—it was a copy of Mack's death certificate.

—

"Look here," I said, standing next to him and pointing to the page. "See, this is how it says he died. Hemopericadium. See? 'Stab/incised to chest.' A knife through the heart. That's how my husband died. Imagine what it was like finding that out. Getting this report and seeing that. A knife through his heart. His huge heart. And he got a knife right there."

Brian didn't say anything. He just stared at the paper.

"I watched him die, man. My husband died in my arms. And there's no way I can describe to you how horrible that was."

I remembered how heavy Mack's body felt in my arms when he sank to the ground next to the truck. And then his eyes closing. And the blood just soaking through his white tee shirt. "Help me!" I was screaming. "Help!"

"We were there in that apartment complex," I said to Brian, "because Mack wanted to go there to slap somebody and leave. That's what he told me back at our house. I mean, we were in for the night. We'd had our Friday night out, and we were home now. We were safe. I had to pick up Paige in the morning from Mack's mother. I wasn't feeling good from those anxiety attacks. 'You're not going anywhere,' I told Mack. But he wouldn't listen. He was going and that was it. And I couldn't let him go alone and get another DUI and wind up in jail.

"So we get to the apartment complex somewhere after midnight, I guess, and Mack goes to the door of this one place looking for the guy who did him wrong—the guy had accused him of being a narc. And this really big woman came to the door and cursed Mack. Just cursed him right there. 'You're gonna let her talk to me this way?' Mack asked me. I just backed up, shaking my head. 'I'm not fightin' anybody. This is your deal.'

"Then the guy Mack was looking for came outside, and they started fighting. And soon these other guys came out and got in on it. They were all on this patch of grass kind of in front of the building, just whaling on each other. Mack would knock one guy down; then another one would come at him and Mack would take a hit. It just looked like mayhem. 'This is enough!' I was yelling. 'You told me you were coming over here to slap him in the face and then we were leaving!' But they just kept going.

"Finally things seemed to calm down—the fighting stopped. Guys were milling around, kind of staring at each other. It became less hectic. People started getting in their cars and leaving. It had to have been around three in the morning, and I thought for sure we were done. But then I saw Mack walk over to the truck and get out this wood pole he always carried with him.

" 'Okay,' he yelled, 'who wants some now?'

"I just about lost it. 'Mack,' I begged him, 'we have *got* to go! This is insane! You've said your piece. You've done your damage here. Let's go!' But he wouldn't listen to me.

"Then I saw people coming out of the apartment with bottles and grill tops, and I knew it was not going to be good. 'No!' I was yelling. And all those people just crowded around Mack, and right away they got the best of him. I turned away for a second, and when I looked over again, he was on the ground.

" 'Get away from him!' I yelled. Everything was happening so fast. I was trying to get to the truck, get Mack to listen to me, stay away from the fight, avoid getting run over as people were leaving. I couldn't focus. Then I turned away again and started yelling at some people across the parking lot. 'Help him! Do something!' But when I turned back to the fight, everything had changed. People were scattering. There was this weird quiet. And Mack was still lying on the ground.

"In a minute, he moved a little, got himself up, and began walking toward the truck. He was walking really slowly. In my mind I was thinking, 'Okay, he's gotten the crap beat out of him, but he's finished now. We're going home.' But then I could see that something was wrong with him. He just looked weak. He got to the truck and opened the door and tried to pull himself up to get in, but he couldn't do it. He was just barely holding onto that door.

"'Mack!' I yelled. I ran over to him, and he collapsed right there in my arms. And his eyes closed immediately.

"'Honey, what's wrong? What's wrong?' He wouldn't answer me.

"'Honey? Honey! What is it, what's wrong?' Then I looked down and saw all this blood coming through his tee shirt. 'Help me!' I yelled. I lifted up the shirt, and there was the wound and blood just everywhere. I thought maybe somehow those guys had turned Mack's stick on him or something. But later I found out what it was—a knife. There was no way a stick could've done that.

"So I yelled for these two friends. 'Come help me! He's hurt! Pick him up and put him in the back of the truck. We've got to get him to the hospital.' We lifted Mack and put him in the truck bed. I got in and started driving. But we only made it a few yards to the stop sign before the cops pulled up. I was just hysterical. 'Help us!' I screamed, jumping out of the truck. 'Something's wrong with my husband! Y'all have to get an ambulance! Get him to the hospital!'

"They pulled him out of the truck and we sat there. And you know what, Brian? We sat there for probably twenty minutes waiting on the ambulance. I know now that it wouldn't have made any difference, because he died when he was in my arms. But sitting in that parking lot, I was just going, 'Why couldn't I have driven him to the hospital myself?'

"I remember the paramedics hooking Mack up to a machine that kept saying, 'Give more air. Breathe. Give more air. Breathe. Give more air.'

"'Give him some more air!' I was yelling. 'Help him breathe!' I was thinking about Paige. In just a few hours I was supposed to go get her. Just a few hours. If he could just hold on. To see her. To see Paige.

"But they took him away. And they wouldn't even let me identify his body. They just put him in the ambulance, and I didn't see him again until I buried him. A paramedic asked, 'Mrs. Smith, how long were y'all married.' I said, 'Two and a half years.' Then he said, 'We're sorry, he's gone.'

"'Where'd he go?' I asked, not understanding. 'Where did he go?'"

Brian was holding the death certificate at his side now. He was watching me, looking in my eyes. And I knew he was hearing every word I said.

"Did anyone ever pay for it?" he asked.

"No," I said, taking a deep breath. "No, they didn't."

"They didn't? No one got caught?"

"No. They all ran off in the woods, and the police never found the knife. A couple of guys were held and then released. But no. No one has ever paid."

I remembered something Paige had asked me. "Mommy, where are those people who killed Daddy?" How was I supposed to answer that? Almost four years and no one had paid. What was I supposed to say? "Well, honey, they're out enjoying their lives right now"? I couldn't say that. So I just said what I believed, what I hoped. "The police are working on it, Angel. They'll find those people. Don't you worry."

"Here's Mack," I said to Brian now, reaching over to the bar and grabbing a small pewter picture frame. Mack was standing up and holding Paige in the living room of our house. He was really tan and wearing a white tee shirt, some khakis, and a brown leather belt. He and Paige were looking at the camera. Mack was smiling. Paige looked stunned. And they both had that same little pug nose.

I held the frame out for Brian to see. "Yep, this is Mack and Paige. That must've been the summer before he died. He died August 18, 2001."

Brian looked at the picture and shook his head.

"But you know," I said, "they just took Mack away from that parking lot. I tried to get over to the ambulance, but the police were questioning me, and they said, 'We're putting you in the car.'

"'Can't I see him?' I asked. 'No,' they said. 'Somebody else can identify his body.' And I'm like, 'But I'm his wife.' Still they wouldn't let me go. They said they didn't want me to touch him. And they took me into the station for like two hours and drilled me with questions. I remember saying to my mom, 'Just please go get my Xanaxes.' From that point on I didn't want to feel anything.

"Then later the coroner called and said, 'Your husband was stabbed to death through the heart.' And I was like, 'What?' That was the first I'd heard of a knife. All I could think of was Mack's huge heart and a knife going through him there and how horrible it was. And then I thought of Paige. I just kept thinking about what she would have to go through.

"I was staying at my aunt's house then, and everybody there was talking about a funeral, and I was just like, 'This is not happening to me.' The story kept coming up on the news, and I saw Mack's truck on TV, because they wouldn't let me take it. And I kept hearing 'fight' and 'Mack Smith.' And I'm like, 'This is not happening.' I couldn't handle it. When one Xanax would wear off, I'd just take another one.

"And when we had the funeral, people were walking in and going, 'What did they do to his head? Why did they cut his head open?' Somebody said, 'Well, they had to do an autopsy.' I didn't understand any of that. I mean, that's not the first time I'd been to a funeral, but as far as an autopsy goes—I didn't know what they did.

"So here I'm handed this death certificate—that thing you have in your hand now—and I'm thinking, 'I've lost everything. My provider, my best friend, my daughter's father. Just everything. What do I have to go on? Nothing. I can't raise her without him. That was what we fought for throughout our whole marriage—to be together for her. To make it for her. To be a family. How am I going to live now?'

"Brian, that's what I was faced with. That's what I went through. And the wife of that agent you killed is going through that same thing now. She's gonna get a death certificate too. She'll wonder why this is happening to her. She'll read the cause of death. The time of death. All of it. All of that horrible stuff. Just like I did."

22 making a move

I set the picture of Mack and Paige back on the bar and took the death certificate out of Brian's hand. I knew he had heard what I said to him. I knew he was listening to every word. He didn't say anything, but it seemed that he was really starting to feel my feelings and know who I was. *What he does with all that is his choice, God. Just keep working with me here. Keep showing me what to do.*

"Can I—?" he started. "Do you mind if I stay here for a few days? You know, just stay here and relax for a few days and then I'll do it—turn myself in."

Wow. "Sure," I said. "I guess, yeah. You can stay here."

I wasn't telling him no. I mean, I knew I wasn't staying here with him. I was leaving to go see Paige. And after I left here, he was going to have to make some choices. He couldn't just chill out in my apartment while the whole world was looking for him. He had to pay for what he did. And he really needed to make the decision to do that now. He needed to go on and do it. I didn't want there to be a big shoot-out in front of my apartment and people dying.

"I just need a few days," he said again. "You know, to relax, smoke some pot, drink some beer."

"Okay," I said. "Sure."

I had no idea where he thought he was going to get any pot. Did he think I would get it for him? Was he going to force me to stay here?

No. I couldn't think that way. I was leaving—I really felt he was going to let me—and at least he was talking about turning himself in now. He just needed to do it sooner. If he waited, he might change his mind. And if he changed his mind, then he would need money, and then he'd have to hurt someone to get it.

"I've gotta make a move," Brian said again now. *He keeps saying that. What is he talking about—a move? What, are we playing a chess game here or something?*

"I have to get rid of this truck," he explained. "It's gonna be daylight soon, and I need to take this truck somewhere before they find it. And look, you're gonna have to pull me out of here, okay? Are you familiar with this area? Do you know anywhere around here, you know, where I could leave the truck?"

I couldn't think. "I mean, I'm kind of familiar with it," I said. "Not really, though." *So he wants me to lead him to ditch the truck? I have no idea where to tell him. Maybe I could say I'm not going. But then those guns are in there.*

"What about breakfast?" I asked him, pointing toward the kitchen. I just wanted to stay here and cook. "I was about to fix it."

"No," he said. "I've gotta move now. It's almost daylight."

I figured I needed to cooperate with him. I didn't want to make him feel that he had to threaten me, and I knew he wasn't playing when it came to ditching that truck. If I didn't agree to help him, I thought, one of two things could happen. He could say, "I don't need you anymore," and just kill me. Or he could leave, and the police would never find him—or it would take longer—and then someone else would get hurt. I was feeling like he really was going to let me leave to go see Paige, so I needed to just keep cooperating. Plus, I knew that if we dropped off the truck, then he wouldn't have a car anymore once I left at 9:30.

"Okay," I said. "We'll go." I looked across the kitchen at the microwave and could just make out the clock—it read 6:45.

I walked back to my closet with the death certificate now and slid it back in that box on top of my file drawers. *I've got to change clothes real quick.*

I stuck my head out the closet door and listened. I could hear him moving around in the living room, so I closed the double doors and looked at my clothes. *Don't let him come in here. Some sweats. There they are.* I grabbed my navy blue Adidas sweats with the white stripes down the sides. Then I pulled down a red Georgia Bulldogs sweatshirt from the rack. I dropped them both on the floor in front of me and got out of my jeans as fast as I could. Then I pulled the sweats on. *Okay.*

Working my feet into a pair of tennis shoes now, I pulled the sweatshirt on over my tank top and finally walked out of the closet, pushing the doors behind me. On my way out of the room, I grabbed a hair band off my dresser and pulled my hair back in a ponytail. *Ready now. I can't believe I'm headed out the door with this guy.*

Brian was standing in the living room wearing his big red jacket and my brown leather clogs again. His feet were hanging way off the back.

Suddenly, I remembered my cell phone—it was still sitting on the glass column table. *I really want that phone.* For some reason I felt like I could just ask him for it. I didn't know why. I mean, what if he flipped out and quit trusting me and then didn't let me leave? But I wasn't really afraid of that happening. I just figured I might as well ask. He had been listening to me talk about my life for hours. He knew what I wanted him to do. He was telling me he would do it—turn himself in—in a few days. I just thought I would take the risk. So I asked.

"Can I take my cell phone with me?" *Please don't let him get mad.*

"Do you want to take your phone?" he asked. He didn't look irritated or anything—he just seemed matter-of-fact about it.

"Yeah," I said. "I do." Actually, I didn't know at that point what I was going to do with my phone. I didn't necessarily think it would be good to call 911, because then there could be violence, and I really believed, especially with the way he was talking now, that he was going to let me leave. But I wanted the option to make that call. I would feel safer with my phone.

"All right," he said. He reached into his jacket pocket and handed me something—it was the battery. "Here. I took the battery out earlier as a precaution."

"Okay," I said, taking it from him. "Thanks."

Was this actually happening? He was letting me take my phone with me in my car? And he was giving me back the battery? *Man, I really do have this guy's trust here. Something huge must be happening inside of him.* But what did it mean? What did he think I wanted the phone for? I mean, didn't he think I would call the police? Did he *want* me to call the police? Did he want *me* to turn him in? I didn't know, but picking the phone up off the table, I thought I needed to be very smart about this.

Just then I stepped over to the kitchen to turn off the overhead light, and as I was about to hit the switch, I noticed something. There was one Xanax sitting out on the red place mat next to the microwave. The pill was sitting in front of the picture of Paige; it was the last pill in a bottle I had had for months now. I had thrown the bottle out the day I moved in and just set that one pill on the counter there. I hadn't really seen it again until now. Quickly I went and reached for it and stuck it in my mouth.

"What's that?" Brian asked. He was standing near the foyer watching me across the bar. I grabbed a glass out of the cabinet, filled it at the sink, and drank a couple of swallows.

I really just thought that pill would help me a little. I was exhausted. My emotions were everywhere. We were about to leave the house and ditch a truck this guy had stolen from a man he had killed. I'd been dealing with this guy for hours. And I just felt like I could use that Xanax. I didn't really think I had a problem with Xanax anymore. When I was addicted to pills, I'd go through a bottle in a month or less. I didn't do that now. Not even close. Of course, a drug addict shouldn't be taking anything—nothing; but right then I just took it.

"It's Xanax," I said to him, wiping my mouth on my sleeve. "It's for anxiety."

I grabbed my pocketbook off the coffee table and my keys where they were lying on Paige's toy box, and we walked out the front door. I was still holding the phone and the battery in my hand. It was dark out—the outside lights around the building were still turned on—but not totally dark. Not pitch black. I could see the sun just barely beginning to light up. *Not too much longer, Lord. Just help me hold on a little longer.*

My car was parked at the end of the sidewalk where I had left it several hours before to make the run for my front door. Maybe three car lengths away, the agent's blue truck was backed into that parking space directly behind me. For a second I remembered it all: Sitting at the wheel. Knowing someone was sitting behind me in that truck. Getting my keys ready. Deciding to make a run for it. Opening my car door. Stepping onto the pavement. Then hearing that click. His door. He was coming.

"Lead the way," Brian said now, leaving me at my car door and walking to the truck.

I was thinking back to that moment he grabbed me. I could hear his voice. "Stop screaming! If you stop screaming, I won't hurt you. Just shut up!" I felt like he was going to kill me right then. Just blow my head off. Right there. "My little girl doesn't have a daddy, and if you hurt me she won't have a mommy." I was thinking about all of that now. It seemed like an eternity ago. And this guy seemed totally different to me. Totally different. Like, I just knew he was going to let me leave. And I was really beginning to believe he was going to turn himself in.

Brian was in the truck now and had just started it up. Standing at my blue Bonneville, I put the key in, swung open the heavy door, and got in. The light blue upholstery reeked of cigarettes. That Hello Kitty air freshener on my gearshift was just worthless. *Where am I taking him, God? I have absolutely no idea. Where does someone ditch a truck around here?*

I backed out and drove down around the building to the first stop sign. About five hours ago I had done this same thing, thinking I was going out for cigarettes, coming right back home, and going to bed. I was thinking about sleep right now, too. Thursday night I'd only gotten a few hours because I did that ice, stayed up all night moving, and then went to bed from dawn until the time my step-dad woke me up, calling about Brian Nichols. I hadn't been to sleep since.

At the stop sign I took a right and started toward one of the exits from the complex. I looked in my rearview mirror to check on Brian. Then I reached over to the passenger's seat where I had laid the cell phone and the battery. I was going to try to put this thing together with one hand while watching the road. I didn't want Brian to look at me from behind and think I was up to something. I didn't see him take a gun out of the house; I didn't think he had one. But I didn't know. And I had this fear that if he thought I was calling the police, he might commit suicide right there in the truck. So I worked with the phone one-handed, and I got the battery in.

When I reached the apartment complex exit, I made a left on West Liddell Road and drove up to the stoplight at Old Norcross Road. The first time I made a drug run to Atlanta with John, we went to a drug dealer's house somewhere on Old Norcross. *Just thank you, God, all that is over. Done. Behind me. Thank you I didn't do those drugs in that bathroom. Thank you I'm still alive. Thank you for just letting me be out here in this car by myself right now. Just, thank you.*

I turned left on Old Norcross, a two-lane road with a lot of trees and curves and hills, now heading southwest, just above and vaguely parallel to I-85. I was driving in a kind of exhausted Xanax haze. I looked in my rearview mirror, and there was Brian. I had no idea where to take him or what kind of setting he wanted for the truck. What was I doing? *What do you want me to do here, God? I'm out here in my car. Do I call the police now? Do I just try to kind of drive off, drive away from him?*

With my piece of junk for a car, I knew the idea of trying to outrun the truck was just stupid. That would never work, and I wouldn't feel safe attempting it. But what about the police? I didn't know if I should do that—call them right now. If I called 911, then Brian could drive off and he'd be on the run again. There could be a terrible scene and people could die—he could die. Or he could get away and stay on the run and hold more people hostage or rob the bank, and even more people would get hurt. It just didn't seem like a good idea. I knew this guy was going to let me leave at 9:30. I just knew it. He trusted me. He had let me take this phone. He was talking about turning himself in now. He just wanted a place to relax for a few days. Shouldn't I wait it out? I didn't know what to do.

After going through a few lights on Old Norcross, I came to a road that looked like it led into a subdivision: Millerbrook Drive. I put my blinker on and hung a right. Brian was right behind me. Immediately, we were in a subdivision of houses all sitting really close together. I took my first left and turned into a cul-de-sac that ended in a long wooden fence. It was just a short road with a few houses on each side. I drove down to the end. In my rearview mirror I could see Brian drive past the cul-de-sac and make a U-turn.

Okay. So I guess this isn't what he wanted. I pulled into a driveway, turned around, and drove back up to Millerbrook Drive. Brian had the truck pointed back in the direction of Old Norcross Road now, and he was sitting just to my left as I came out of the cul-de-sac. I could see his passenger-side window was down.

I rolled down my window to see what he wanted. "I'm not parking here," he said. I was close enough to him that he didn't have to yell. "Somebody will find it here. They'll find this place. Follow me."

I let him pull in front of me, and he led us back up to the intersection with Old Norcross. Then he took a right, and we continued back in the direction I had us going in the beginning. I didn't see many cars on the road. I glanced down at my phone again. *What do I do here?* I decided to dial 911 and just not hit send for a minute. I knew if I called the police, I would have to put the phone up to my ear, and if he looked at me in his rearview mirror, he would say, "Yeah, she's calling the police." *Should I do it? God, just show me what to do.*

Old Norcross Road began to take a slight turn downhill to the right as we came up on a major intersection at Buford Highway. *Where's he taking us? He doesn't know where we're going, either.* Then, right before we got to the light, Brian put on his left blinker. He was turning us onto a little cut-through road behind the CVS Pharmacy and jetting us up to Buford Highway that way. When we got up there, up to Buford

Highway, he went slightly right; then he cut across Buford Highway to a road that appeared to go into a kind of industrial park area. There were a bunch of warehouse-looking buildings with loading docks. Everything looked completely deserted. *How did he find this place?*

Maybe a few blocks of buildings down the industrial road, Brian put on his right blinker. We were turning into this empty parking lot just in front of a row of brick buildings. Brian drove the truck all the way down to the end, where there was a tree line. All the parking spaces were on the left-hand side next to the row of buildings. Then he turned to the right a little and backed the truck into the last parking space on the row. A brick building with the letter "A" on it was right behind the truck now, and a hedge or some shrubs were to the left. I pulled my car in next to the truck; then I backed up so my passenger door was right next to him.

Am I about to do this? Am I actually letting him in my car and going back to that apartment? Brian got out of the truck. It looked like he might have something under his red coat now—there was a small bulge, like maybe he got something out of the truck that he didn't have before. *A gun?* I had no idea. *Okay. He's out here. I could just drive off now and leave him. I could jam my foot on this accelerator and go and call the police.*

But no—I just couldn't see doing that. Either he'd take the truck and start running again. Or the police would come, and a lot more people would die. And what if I called the police and then let him into my car to keep him from running? The cops would have to surround Brian and me together, and *I* could get hurt. No. I really believed if I just got him back to my apartment, then he would let me leave to go see Paige. He would let me leave and then he wouldn't have a car. He wanted to rest, he said. He was tired of hurting people. And I was so tired at this point, I almost felt like I couldn't think anymore. *I'm just sticking with the original plan here, Lord. Just please, please protect me.*

At that moment Brian walked up to the passenger door and opened it. He got in, shut that heavy door, and looked over at me for a second. "Man," he said. "You really *are* a 'ride or die chick.'"

23 saturday breakfast

"So," I asked him, pulling out of the parking lot onto that industrial park road, "are you ready now?"

"For what?" he asked. I could tell out of the corner of my eye that he was looking at me.

"To turn yourself in," I said. I was just going to be matter-of-fact about this stuff now, like I was taking it for granted that he was going to do it. He was turning himself in and that was all. And I seriously felt right then that he might possibly tell me, "Sure, yeah. Go ahead. Let's go to the courthouse." I really thought he might say that.

"No," he said, turning away from me. "No, I just need a few more days." *Okay, so is he not moving off this "few more days" thing? Doesn't he know he can't wait a few more days? He could change his mind if he waits, and things could get worse.*

Then he said, "If you give me a few more days, I'll let you take me to the courthouse and turn myself in and then everybody's just gonna praise you and talk about how wonderful you are."

I didn't say anything. But I was thinking, "Look, buddy, I'm not planning on being around in a few more days to do that, okay? And I don't care about that anyway. I don't care about people saying how wonderful I am because it's not me doing this. I know who's doing it, and it sure isn't me."

We drove in silence back the way we came: the cut-through street to Old Norcross Road to West Liddell. We passed a few cars on the road. "If they only knew," I thought, glancing at the drivers as the cars went by. "If they only knew who was driving past them." *I wish I was in their position. I really wish all of this was just over.*

Finally, I turned back into the apartment complex and took the long road up to my section of buildings. My section was set off a little bit from the rest of the apartments. The road kind of curved and went over a short bridge with stone handrails—there was a creek there and a grassy area—and then it kept going up behind some three-story apartment buildings on the right and left.

After we crossed the creek, I took the only right turn, then curved around to the left to my building—the first building. All the buildings were on the left. Driving now, I was thinking again about how unbelievable it was that this guy had ended up at my place. Two days ago—well, three now—I had lived clear on the other side of this apartment complex. And driving through it, I saw again how many apartments were out here. The place was just huge to me.

I pulled the car into my same parking space. By now it was really starting to get light out; I was guessing it was somewhere around 7:30. It wasn't fully daylight, but I could see things clearly now—cars, trees, the rails around people's porches, the rail around my porch, and the boxes sitting out there from the move. I could see it all. And I was really glad about it. Because I was that much closer to 9:30.

"Wait," Brian said now. I was just about to open my door and get out. He was looking out his window. Five or six cars away from us, a woman was coming out of her apartment in the last building.

"Just wait," he said again. I waited like he asked.

Maybe I could've done something then—like called out to that woman for help. Maybe I could've taken that opportunity. But there was just no way I could see doing that right then. I wasn't going to freak Brian Nichols out. We were already at my apartment, and he was going to let me leave. I just wasn't risking the total nightmare of this guy breaking down and going inside and getting those guns and losing it out here. I had to stick with my plan.

I unlocked the door for us and went straight to the kitchen. This was a great time for breakfast—I was starving. "Hungry now?" I asked as he came in behind me.

"Yeah, I am." He unzipped his coat and kicked off those clogs. *So maybe there wasn't anything in his coat.* Then he shoved both the shoes and the coat under the coffee table.

I turned on the burner under my pancake pan and poured a little oil in there. Then I got the mixing bowl down and opened up the box of pancake mix.

Brian was looking at the photographs on the bar. There were two big eight-by-ten silver frames, one on either end—one of Paige, one of my eleven-year-old sister, Leah. There were several smaller frames in between. Pictures of Paige, some of me, one of my family at my cousin's wedding, the picture of Mack holding Paige, and others. There was another framed eight-by-ten of Paige sitting on the stereo speaker next to the dresser where the TV was—I had just put that frame out before all of this started last night; Paige was holding a red flower.

"Are all these you?" Brian asked. I turned around and saw him leaning over the agent's tools to look closely at the pictures on the bar. There was a black-and-white photo of me wearing those extensions in my hair and others with me wearing my hair sometimes straight, sometimes curly like it was now.

"Yep," I said. "They're all me. It's my hair—it can be straight or curly."

"Well, I like it better curly," he said, still bent over looking. *Okay. Cool. Whatever. That's fine.*

Then he asked, "Can I see some more pictures of your family?" I was cracking eggs into the pancake mix now.

"Sure," I said. *He must really be feeling close to me if he wants to see family pictures.*

I rinsed off my hands in the sink and dried them quickly. Then I walked around the bar where he was standing and went to the dresser. I kept a bunch of loose photos in the top drawer, so I just reached in there and grabbed a stack. "Come in here and I'll show them to you," I said.

He followed me into the kitchen, and I stood next to him flipping through the pictures. "Here's Paige and me and my mom at my cousin Sarah's wedding. Here's my cousin Rebekah. This is Mack and me and Paige in our Easter picture—we took one every Easter. We're out at his parents' trailer in this one."

"Can I hold them?" Brian asked. *Wow, God. What are you doing here with this guy? He wants to hold them?*

"Sure, okay." I handed him the stack of pictures and went back to mixing up my pancake batter.

"Who's this?" he asked now. He had stepped over closer to me and was holding the picture out.

"That's my mom with my little brother and sister, Christian and Leah. My mom had them with my step-dad when I was fourteen. Christian's a top-level gymnast, and Leah's a really passionate reader."

I went to the stove with the bowl of batter now and dropped my first pancake into the pan. "And that—" I said, trying to kind of pay attention to the pictures he was looking at, "that's at recovery right there. All of those you're looking at right there are recovery. I went last year from January to April. Before that, I'd gone to these two other programs and kind of just failed or dropped out early or whatever. I just didn't want it. And you can't recover that way. You've got to want it.

"See that one there," I said, "with me sitting on the back of that truck with all those bales of pine straw?" I was trying to watch for the pancake to start bubbling so I could flip it.

"Well," I told him, "I went to recovery knowing I had to go. I was willing and everything. But at first I just hated it. All I wanted to do was sleep. It was like depression, not having drugs, knowing I couldn't have drugs, and everything else was going down on me at once. But later I ended up being made pine crew leader and that's what those pictures are showing—us working out in the pine forest.

"We went to this forest—there, in that next picture you can see it—and we had to rake rows of pine straw and gather it all together, roll it up, and then take it to the truck so they could drive it to this big pile where we would bale it. We'd be out there working in ten-degree weather. No sun was coming through because the pine trees were blocking it. We would wear two pairs of gloves, and our hands would be frozen. Just cold, cold, cold, cold."

I looked at my pancake again now, and it was bubbling like crazy. I grabbed the spatula to flip it. "Man, I burned it," I said, reaching for a pot holder across the counter. I picked up the pan, carried it over to the laundry closet in the far left-hand corner of the kitchen, and opened the door; then I flipped the pancake into the trash can. "Gotta pay more attention, I guess." *What's the deal? I never burn pancakes.*

I started another one while he was still going through the pictures. "And you know," I told him, "my whole entire life changed at that recovery." I was touching the edges of the pancake with my spatula now.

"I got back in touch with the Lord there. Everything they taught me really sank in. You know, deal with your own problems. Don't blame them on anything else. Don't blame them on anybody else. It's your fault. You did it. That kind of thing. And like, I was so angry at Mack for not listening to me the night he got stabbed, because if he would have listened to me, then he wouldn't have died, and none of this would have happened to me. That's what I thought, anyway.

"But see," I said, turning from the stove now to look at Brian, "I had to face that whole way of thinking. I had to face it and admit that certain things happened to me because I chose to do those drugs—and because I didn't choose to turn to God and say, 'Help. What do I do now?'"

"We're almost ready," I told Brian. He was still in the kitchen, not really looking at my pictures anymore. He was just watching me cook. Just listening. Not saying a word.

I had several pancakes done now—they were sitting on a plate next to the stove—and I was scrambling up some eggs in a skillet. "Just another minute or two," I told him.

I got a couple of my glass plates down from the cabinet and put some pancakes on one for him. Then I stirred the eggs a few more times and picked up the pan with the pot holder so I could scoop some eggs onto his plate.

"Here's yours," I said, handing him the plate. "Go sit down at the table, and I'll get the rest of the stuff. Oh, wait! Here's a napkin." I grabbed a couple of paper towels off the roll and handed them to him.

He took his plate into the dining room. My table and chairs were on the other side of the fridge, so I couldn't see him anymore. But I could hear him set his plate down on the glass tabletop.

Next I made a plate for myself and went and set that out on the table. Brian was sitting on the side nearest that big mattress and box springs. He hadn't started yet—I hadn't given him any silverware.

"Sorry. I'm almost ready. I'm bringing your silverware." I went back to the kitchen, took down a couple of glasses, and got a bottle of Minute Maid fruit punch out of the fridge. I poured the drinks—I gave him the Disney World glass—and took those out. Then I went and grabbed the syrup and the butter dish out of the fridge and some silverware out of the drawer.

"Wow," he said, as I set the things down carefully on the glass table. "Real butter? Pancakes?"

"Yeah," I said. "Hope you enjoy it." *Real butter? He's impressed by this stuff? Dude, this is real life. People eat butter. People eat pancakes. He just isn't doing that well right now, is he?*

Finally, I sat down to eat with him. I grabbed one of the paper towels and put it in my lap. Then I just closed my eyes for a second. *Thank you, God, for this food. And thank you for bringing me this far.*

I waited on Brian to fix his pancakes with butter and syrup, and then I fixed mine—I used lots of both. It was Saturday morning. This was what I used to do every Saturday morning. Every Saturday in another life. Now Mack was gone and Aunt Kim was fixing Paige's breakfast. And I was sitting here over pancakes with Brian Nichols.

"How is it?" I asked him after he'd taken a few bites.

"It's great, really great," he said, sipping his juice.

I cut into my stack of pancakes and took my first bite. I thought, "Honestly, Ashley, these are the best pancakes you've ever made in your life right here." I didn't know. Just something about them. They were incredible.

Then Brian looked up and said, "You know, Ashley, I wish I would've met you at a different time and under different circumstances. We could've been friends."

I smiled a little. I didn't really know what to say—or what to feel. I knew after hearing those words that he would let me leave. I was also thinking about his child, and how he was going to prison now and wouldn't get to raise him. I felt bad for Brian. But then I remembered the agent and his family, and the other families, and what they would have to go through—what they were already going through. And I started to feel tired, so tired and sick over that.

We ate for a few minutes in silence, and as our forks clinked against the glass plates, I glanced over at Brian, trying to read his face. He seemed, I don't know, kind of content. Relaxed, maybe. He was eating some real food after all that time in jail, and I knew what that food in there was like. But he still looked melancholy, basically the way he had looked all night. I hoped he was thinking about everything I had told him and what he needed to do now. I knew I didn't have much time left to get through to him. I was leaving soon, and I really didn't want to leave him here by himself. I wanted him to turn himself in while he could still see that it was the right thing to do.

"You know," I said now. "Just think about how far you've traveled these last I-don't-know-how-many hours. You made it out of the courthouse. You made it all the way to Duluth. You made it to this apartment. And now you're sitting here eating breakfast. Can you believe the miracle of that?" I just wanted to keep going back to the miracle thing to remind him he had a reason for being here.

He kept eating, working on his pancakes and eggs. Then he said, "Well, God probably led me right to you. I'm lost right now, and maybe God led me to you to tell me about the families—just, you know, to let me know how they felt. Because you've gone through it yourself."

He wasn't looking at me. He just kept turning his food over with his fork. I felt blown away by what he had just said. He was getting it, totally getting it. *God, he's got to come with me now. He can't stay here.*

"Dude, why don't you just go turn yourself in now?" I said. "I'll drive you up there. We can just go up there and do it. Let me take you. Don't wait a few more days. I mean, you need to do it now, or something really bad might happen. More people could get hurt. You could get hurt. Come on, let me take you."

I cut into my pancakes with my fork and watched him.

"I just need a few more days," he said, still looking at his plate. "I just want to stay here a few more days and relax and eat some real food." *He's really not budging on this. Not budging at all.*

"But, I mean, you just said you're here in this apartment for a reason," I told him. "You got out of that courthouse with police everywhere. Don't you think you're supposed to be sitting in front of me listening to me tell you what you need to do right now?" I just wanted him to see it so badly. *I can't make him, God. I can't make him listen to me.*

I stopped for a minute and took a few bites of my pancakes, trying to enjoy them.

"You know," I said, "Your miracle could be that you go on and pay for this. That you turn yourself in right now and go to prison and share the Word of God with all the other people in there. Maybe that's your purpose right there. Maybe that's what God wants you to do, and he brought you here to my apartment so you could know that. I mean, listen—we could go right now."

He didn't say a word. I could see he just wasn't moving on this at all. *God, I'm trying here, but I don't know what else to say. I've said everything I know. It's his choice, and I can't do any more. You've just gotta help him make the right decision.*

I looked over at Brian's plate now. He'd cleaned it up pretty good. I couldn't eat much more, either. "Okay," I said, taking one more big bite of eggs and sliding off the tall chair. "All done?"

"Yeah," he said, getting up. "It was real good. I'll wash these."

"No, man," I told him. "I've got 'em. Don't worry about it. You're fine."

24 staying calm

I took the plates and put them in the sink, and Brian followed with the syrup and butter and set those on the counter. Then he went and got his glass and brought it over to the bar. He was looking at those pictures again, leaning over the tools. *Maybe he just wants some normalcy in his life right now. Breakfast. Washing dishes. Looking at family pictures.* My heart went out to him.

I could see he was looking at this one picture of my whole family at my cousin Sarah's wedding. It was in a wooden frame that read "The Gang." "Okay," I said, leaving the plates. "Let me show you who those people are."

I went around the bar, picked up the picture, and stood next to him with it. "This is my cousin Israel, and he's a great discus thrower. And this is my cousin Steven, and he goes to East Carolina University, which is in Greenville, North Carolina, and he plays college football there."

"Oh," Brian said, setting his glass on the bar. "Really?" *Good. A point of connection for him. Maybe that helped.*

"And then, here's my cousin Sarah's new husband, Jordan. He plays baseball for Georgia Tech, and we're really hoping he'll go pro. And these are the aunt and uncle that Paige stays with—my Uncle Steve's a doctor, a radiologist, which is why I wanted to go into some type of medicine. And then my brother and my sister again." I just kept on, naming everybody.

I turned back to the bar. "There's my oldest cousin Rebekah holding Paige," I said, pointing to another frame. "And you've already seen the one of Mack and Paige. So, yeah. That's my family right there. Look at those all you want."

I left Brian at the bar and went back around to the sink to start washing dishes. I turned the water on hot and let it run. I got the pans off the stove and then the mixing bowls off the counter. By now it was after eight o'clock. *Not too much longer. Just an hour or so.* I was glad I had something I could be doing. Something where I could be standing up and moving around. I was about to get this kitchen really clean—that's how I liked it anyway. I usually never left a dirty dish in the sink.

As I was working, Brian turned around and went back to the hallway. I saw him go into the bathroom. I still had the water running, but right away I started hearing something strange. Some clattering on the counter. Then a loud clicking noise. I turned the water down a little and listened.

"Click. Click. Click. Click." *The guns. Whoa! What's he doing?* I could feel my whole body just tense up immediately. *Is he coming in here to kill me? Is he about to kill himself?* I stood there frozen: Prepared to see him standing in the doorway pointing a gun. Prepared for the shot. I could hear it in my mind. Just hear the gun going off. Like when he first came in. Like when I was walking to the bathroom. At the beginning. *Please, just let him be taking the bullets out.*

I looked over at the two windows and the door to the porch in the living room. All the blinds were still closed, but I could tell it was really getting light out now. *God, just help me hold on here. I'm so close. I've made it this far. Keep him together for me, God. He's got to let me leave.*

A minute later I saw Brian walk across the hall to my bedroom carrying something. I turned off the water and heard something drop to the floor, some fumbling around. Then he walked out. *There he is.* But his hands were empty. He walked across the room to the TV and turned it on. Then he went back to his spot on the couch and sat down.

"You're gonna be on the news," he said now. I could hear his name on the TV. "Brian Nichols." And all of the same stuff we'd listened to a few hours ago. It was all still playing there on the news.

"What?" I asked him. "On the news?" I didn't get it.

"When I turn myself in and you're out here and I'm in there, you'll be on the news," he said. "And they're gonna want to know everything. So, what will you say to them?"

I was so relieved that he was still talking about turning himself in, I couldn't think for a second. "Well," I said, standing at the sink. "When they want to know, I'll tell them what happened. I'll tell them about the person I saw."

He nodded slowly, looking at me for a second and then turning back to the TV. *What does he think I would say?*

"Look, dude, you came into my house and scared the ever-living crap out of me, but as far as harm me, you didn't harm me." I was thinking about how he hadn't taped up my mouth. How he hadn't raised a hand to me. How he had asked me if that extension cord was too tight. How he had respected me and put that towel over my head.

"I mean, I'm not going to be somebody on TV saying you hit me over the head and did all this stuff to me," I told him. "I'm not gonna, you know, lie and say you did things that you didn't do. Okay?"

I was trying to reassure him—I didn't know what he had been doing in there with those guns. Plus, I wanted him to know that when he did the right thing and turned himself in, I wasn't going to just turn around and make him out to be something he wasn't. I'd already learned all about lying. I'd lied to my family too many times to count. Mainly about drugs. "No, I'm not doing those now." And about people I dated who I knew were losers and druggies. "No, he doesn't do that."

In recovery I wrote everybody letters apologizing for all the lies. For lying and a whole lot more. I'd learned that when you start believing your own lies, you're in deep trouble. And that's where I was when I went into recovery. Every time I tried to make something out to be different than it was, it never came out right. So I was through with that now. I didn't want to be that person anymore. And I hoped Brian could see that.

"What time do you need to leave?" he asked. *Thank you, God.*

"Well," I said, "I have to be there at ten, so I probably need to leave around 9:15 or 9:30." At this point, it was somewhere around 8:30.

"Okay," he said. "So you don't mind if I just stay here a few days and chill out?" *He's asking me again? He just keeps asking me permission for stuff.*

"No, that's fine. You can do that."

"You're sure you don't mind?"

"I don't mind. Sure, go ahead." *Look, if you let me leave here at 9:30, I'm not coming back here to live with you for another three days.*

"Will you come and visit me in jail after I turn myself in?" he asked now. *Wow. He must really think he's found a friend in me if he's asking that.* At least he was still talking like he was going to do the right thing.

"Yes," I said. "Yeah, I'll come and visit you." I wasn't sure at that moment if I would do it or not, but I didn't want to discourage him in any way from what he needed to do.

Then I asked him, "Are you sure you don't want to just come with me when I leave, and I'll take you to the courthouse? I could drive you up there now and you could do it." *Might as well try. Might as well give him every opportunity.*

"No," he said, looking at the TV. "I'll come with you in a few days."

I thought: "He's not going to budge on delaying this thing. And he knows I'm not going to budge on what I think he should do. Maybe he just knows that when I leave I'm making that 911 call, and that's his way of turning himself in. I don't know. I just don't know."

"Can I wash my clothes now?" he asked.

"Yeah, sure," I said. "But you need to fix that washing machine."

Brian got up and went back into my bedroom. I listened. *The guns?* But in a second he came back in the living room carrying his dirty clothes.

"The machine's in there," I said. I was standing next to the bar and the tools, and I pointed toward the far left corner of the kitchen at my laundry room door. I turned and followed him in there.

Brian set his clothes down and pulled the washer back from the wall so he could fix the hook-up. After messing with it for a minute, he pushed the washer back and opened the lid. Some of my clothes were inside—the ones I'd tried to wash right before going out to get cigarettes the night before.

"Do you care if I throw these in with your clothes?" he asked.

"No. I don't care. And there's some laundry detergent right there too." I pointed to the shelf above the machine.

At this point I was just trying to treat him like a roommate. I didn't know what he had done with those guns in my bedroom. He was a huge guy. Things seemed to be going my way, but he could hurt me at any time. And I needed to get out of this apartment. My position with him right here at the end was very, very important.

"Can I wash my face?" I asked him as we walked out of the laundry room. I felt like I needed to ask. He had been letting me do whatever I wanted in the apartment, and he was the one walking around asking me for permission. But I was starting to get anxious and didn't want to do anything to jeopardize my chances of leaving. Just—I knew I didn't have much time left.

"Yeah. Go ahead," he said, taking his seat on the sofa.

I went back into the bathroom now. I hadn't been in here for a while. The guns were gone. The soda bottle, his red baseball hat, the wad of bills from his pants pocket, and the canister of pepper spray were still there on the counter. There was the picture of Paige and me where I'd left it by the sink. The burgundy candle had been blown out, but the small lamp on the counter near the linen cabinet was still on. The overhead light was on. The shower curtain was still partially open. The toilet lid was down. Everything looked pretty much the same.

And that one line of ice was still lying there on the counter with the supermarket card, the rolled-up twenty-dollar bill, my pink zipper pouch, and the tin.

I pulled a fresh hand towel out of the linen cabinet and then got my face soap off the shampoo rack hanging in the shower. There was his washcloth hanging on that rack right next to mine. I looked away—maybe there was blood on it—and went to stand in front of the sink. Then I looked at myself in the mirror. *Wow, you look rough, Ashley. Really bad right now.* I was totally and completely exhausted.

I turned on the water and bent down to wash off the day-old makeup. I could feel myself trying to hurry. I was having this fear right then that while my face was in the sink, he was going to walk up behind me and hit me over the head with something. *Calm down, Ashley. You watch too many movies. He's going to let you leave. Just stay calm.*

I couldn't remember the last time I had washed my face just to wake up, but this morning I knew I needed something. Standing there wiping my face off, I thought, "I just want to lie down so badly, but I've got to keep going." I'd been up all night for basically two nights now. I looked at myself in that sweatshirt and ponytail, and I could hear Aunt Kim and them worrying and saying, "Gosh, look at her! She looks terrible!"

Just then I glanced back over at that line of ice again. There was the twenty-dollar bill. *That's been up his nose, Ashley. Yeah, but it's still twenty bucks. And I'm leaving here. I need that money.* I reached for the bill and shoved it into the pocket of my sweats.

I walked across the hallway to my bedroom. I was just going to be in here for a minute. *Where are those guns? Hurry, Ashley.* I could still hear the TV, and I was guessing Brian hadn't moved from the couch.

Okay. There was the extension cord, the curtain, and that pile of tape thrown over by the dresser. *I know I heard something hit the floor in here.* Looking down, I saw the bed skirt was kind of sticking out funny at the end of the bed, so I knelt down as quietly as I could and lifted the skirt up a little. *There they are. Okay. They're under the bed.* I wasn't sure why he put the guns under there, but maybe it was a good thing. I was hoping it meant he was done. *Lord, please. Please just let him be done.*

I stood up and saw my Bible and *Purpose-Driven Life* book sitting on the bed where I'd left them, so I picked those up. I still had a few minutes to do my devotion before I left, and I was going to do it sitting in the living room. I was sticking to my routine right here. I was giving God his time like I promised him. I hadn't missed a day on this book yet. And anyway, something about my Bible and my book just made me feel comfortable. I wanted them near me. I just wanted them with me in that living room with Brian.

Walking out, I saw one of my closet doors wasn't closed all the way. "My file drawers," I thought. Pushing the closet door shut, I started worrying that when I left, Brian might start going through my paperwork. I mean, what if he decided to keep running and not turn himself in, and he went in there and got my social security number and used it or found a way to steal my identity or something? What could I do? *Ashley, you can't do anything. You have to get out of this apartment. Just stay focused. Be calm. Go sit down.*

"You look really tired," Brian said. I was standing near the bar, facing him and holding my Bible and book.

"Yeah," I said. *Well, what do you think?* "Yes, I am really tired, but the most important thing for me right now is to go and see my daughter. She's waiting on me." I thought I'd better remind him. I was going to see Paige. I was walking out that door. *I'm leaving here, buddy, in about a half hour.*

My glass of juice from breakfast was still sitting on the dining room table, so I went over and picked it up. Then I walked around to my side of the couch and set the glass down on the coffee table.

The TV was still blaring all of that Brian Nichols stuff, but I didn't care now. I was too tired to care. I laid my book beside me on the couch and opened up my Bible.

There was my grandpa's inscription from Christmas 1978 on the inside front cover. "Put Christ first," it read, "—in the home, school, work and play. He will never leave you or forsake you." *That's what I need right now, God. I need you to stay right here with me. Just stay with me.*

I flipped to the back and found Philippians. *Where is it? My verse? There*: "I can do all things through Him who strengthens me." I just sat there looking at the page for a minute. The words all started blurring together. But sitting there with the Bible open made me feel better. *It's just a few more minutes, Ashley. He's going to let you go.*

I reached for my *Purpose-Driven Life* now and opened it to Paige's bookmark. It was still at Day 32, so I flipped ahead to Day 33, "How Real Servants Act." Actually, I hadn't even read Day 32—just that first page with Brian. But it didn't matter now. I couldn't read anyway. I just kept the book open on my lap and stared for a few more minutes at the pages.

25 i'll just be here

I was standing in the kitchen now. The microwave clock read 9:15. Brian was still sitting on the couch in front of the TV, and I was trying to think of what I could do for him—what I could leave around the house to maybe encourage him and keep him focused on what he needed to do.

I had intentionally left my Bible and my book on the coffee table. Maybe he would pick those up and read them. Now I was thinking about the dry-erase board on my fridge. Every morning I tried to write the date on that board, a Bible verse, and a quote from a quote book I used.

I stood at the board now, flipping through a small devotional book looking for a verse. I had gone back to my bedroom and gotten the book out of my basket. Friends of my grandparents had given the book to me about two weeks after Mack died; it was called *God's Inspirational Promise Book*, and I had used it so much, the cover had fallen off. In a moment I found the right verse. *Yes. This right here is definitely the verse he needs.*

I erased the board and wrote "March 12, 2005" at the top in black ink. Then I grabbed the thick blue marker from off the top of the fridge and started writing the verse. I wrote it really big on the board: "So now, those who are in Jesus Christ are not judged guilty. Romans 8:1."

Maybe he would see those words written there the next time he came to the fridge for a beer or something.

"Well, I'm about to leave," I told him. I had come back around the bar now. My pocketbook was sitting on Paige's toy box, where I'd left it after going to drop off the truck, so I stepped over there and picked it up.

I could tell it was really bright outside. The sun was beaming through the cracks in the blinds. It was such a total change from the darkness of the night. Light. Brightness. Morning. Time to go. *Thank you, God.* It was time to go.

"Okay," he said, sitting forward on the couch. "I'll just be here. Will you tell Paige hello for me?"

"Sure," I answered. *What? What am I going to say? "Hey, Paige, Brian Nichols said hello"? My family would really go for that one.*

Then Brian stood up and walked around the corner to the bathroom. He came back a second or two later holding out some cash—the wad of bills from the bathroom counter, I guessed. I wondered if it belonged to the agent.

"Here," he said, holding out the money. "Here's forty bucks."

"No," I said. "No, that's okay. I don't need that." *Man, you better keep that money because if you don't turn yourself in and you start running again, then you're going to hurt someone else trying to steal money, so just keep it.* "Really," I said, "you might need it."

"Just take it," he said, still holding it out. "All I'm going to do is sit here and sleep for the next few days."

My grandmother always told me never to turn down money twice. One time, yes. But not two times. So I just took it—I would figure out who to give it to later. Maybe Brian was giving it to me now because he really was going to turn himself in like he said. I didn't know, but there was no use arguing. I needed to leave.

"Okay," I said, stepping toward him and taking the money.

"Is there anything I can do for you while you're gone?" he asked now. "You know, like hang your curtains or something—or the mirror?" He was pointing to the mirror on the back of the couch. I was going to center it on the wall there and hang a gold angel candleholder on either side.

"Uh, yeah," I said. "You can do that." *I really need to leave here, buddy.* But I could see he was kind of itching to do something. Maybe the drugs were getting to him. Maybe he wanted to help. Whatever it was, he needed something to do right then.

So I said, "The hammer's in the drawer by the stove, and the nails are in a plastic container on that shelf in the laundry room." Right after I said it, he went to go get them.

Then I glanced down at my curtain rod just beside Paige's toy box. Next to it were three of the four panels that were supposed to go on it—the missing cream-colored panel was what Brian had used to tie me up. I grabbed the rod quickly and put those three panels on—tan, cream, tan—and held it out to him as he came back in the room.

"Here," I said, "you can hang this up too over these windows if you want." Then I laid the rod down on Paige's toy box, dug my keys out of my purse, and turned toward the foyer.

I figured Brian knew this was the last time he was going to see me. He had to have known I was going to call the police. He must've known. But if he did, he never let on.

"Okay," I said. "Well, bye." I was standing at one end of the coffee table. He was standing at the other end, holding the hammer and nails.

"Bye," he said. "See you later."

I walked to the door and opened it, and the light just poured in.

26 surrender

Pulling the door closed, I felt like my knees were just going to buckle under me right there. The sun was beaming down on me. It was bright, incredibly bright. And I thought I was going to collapse on the way to the car. I could hardly walk those ten steps. My legs wouldn't move right. My heart was racing. I was trying to think. *Okay, I've got to call the police right now. Right now. What if he opens that door? What if he comes after me? What if he has those guns and shoots me in the back? What if he just blows me away?*

I got to my car as fast as I could without my knees giving out. I had my keys ready and could see my hand shaking as I tried to get the key in the lock. Once I got the door open, I threw my pocketbook to the passenger side, climbed in, and shut the door. I was almost frozen behind the wheel—I couldn't move for a second. For a brief second. Then I put the key in the ignition and started the car. *Thank you, God.*

I backed up and drove around that corner, just yanking stuff out of my purse with my right hand to find my cell phone. *Here it is.* I opened the phone, and when I got down the short hill to that first stop sign, I dialed 911.

It was busy.

"You've got to be kidding me!" I was yelling at the phone. *They've got to go get him right now or he's gonna hurt somebody or hurt himself.* I knew if he hurt himself, I was going to have to walk back into that apartment, and that would just be traumatizing. I couldn't do that. *Lord, be with this whole situation. Help me here.*

Now I was pulling up to the second stop sign, leading out of the apartment complex, and I dialed 911 again.

It was busy again.

"Y'all get off the phone! I've got something really important to say here! This is freakin' nuts!"

I had taken a right on West Liddell and now was turning left at the light onto Satellite Boulevard. There was the QuikTrip up on the right where I'd gone to get cigarettes. And a Shell station on the left. I had dialed 911 a third time. Now it was ringing. And as I got to the next light someone answered. *Well, thank you!*

"Gwinnett County 911," the woman said.

"Hey," I said, trying to get air. "I'm calling because Brian Nichols has been in my house all night long."

"What?"

"Yes, ma'am." I felt pretty calm suddenly. I was able to talk to her. She asked me my name. "Ashley Smith," I said.

Then: "Where are you?"

"I'm on the way to see my daughter." I was headed like I was going to Dacula to my uncle's church. *I just want to see Paige right now. That's all I want to do.*

The woman got me to explain where the apartment was. "It's 3414 Ridge Brook Trail," I told her. "Bridgewater Apartments."

Then she said, "Ma'am, we need you to go back to the leasing office."

I turned around and headed back to the apartment complex. *Do I have to go back there?* I was so exhausted. For a minute I just wanted out of this whole thing. But no. I had to be there. They had to get Brian before something happened. The woman on the phone said the police would meet me at the leasing office. I had her on the line as I drove, and all I could think was, "What's he doing? Has he left? Has he gotten those guns and left? Has he gone through that stuff in my closet? Is he dead?"

The leasing office was a few minutes' drive from my apartment. I pulled into the parking area, and within five to ten seconds, the first police car arrived. The woman with 911 was asking me, "Where are you now? Where are you?"

"They're here," I told her. "I'm walking toward them."

I got to the cop car and just started talking, trying to answer their questions.

"Where is he?" "He's in my apartment. 3414. It's on the bottom level."

"Are you sure it was him?" "Yes, I'm sure." *I just spent the whole entire night with the guy. Yes, yes, I'm sure.*

"What did he look like?" "He's black, tall, pretty big. Look, it was him." *Don't just stand here! Go get him! Don't you understand? Something bad could happen!*

"How did he get here?" "He had a truck."

"What truck?" "I think it was a CIA agent's truck. But he got rid of it. I went with him."

"Ma'am, you've got to take us to that truck." *What? Are they saying they won't believe me unless they see the truck? They'll never get him in time. He could be gone. With all of those guns.*

I got into the backseat of one of the police cars, and we started toward the industrial area where Brian had dropped off the truck a couple of hours earlier.

We went back by the same route I had driven just as it was getting light. West Liddell. Old Norcross. The cut-through street. Crossing Buford Highway. The industrial park road. And then the right-hand turn into that parking lot by the row of brick buildings.

"There it is," I said. There was the dark blue pickup. Right where Brian had left it a little after dawn. In the last parking space next to the hedge and in front of building "A." The last time I had looked at that truck, Brian was opening my passenger door and climbing into my car. *You really are a "ride or die chick."*

"Thank you, ma'am," one of the cops said. He radioed another officer, and over the speaker I heard, "It's him. It's him. He's in our county."

I thought: "I tried to tell y'all. I just spent a bunch of time with the man. I mean, I know it's him. You don't have to doubt me." *Can you guys please just go in and get this guy?*

Back at the apartment complex, we continued on past the leasing office, and I could see police cars driving around the corner toward my apartment—just one car after the next. *Okay, it looks like I'm going back down there. I really don't want to go down there.*

We followed the line of cars down that long road, and I could see they were beginning to set up right there at the bridge. Police cars. Unmarked cars. Vans. A black Tahoe. Police in uniform. Others in plain clothes. Helicopters were flying overhead. *Lord, this is huge. This is huge. Just please don't let there be a blood bath.*

I got out of the car, and immediately different officers started rushing at me. I was the only person who had seen Brian Nichols. I was trying to explain how to get to my apartment. "It's real easy," I said. "It's 3414. All you have to do is go up, take the only right that you can, then go around the corner to the left, and it's the first building on the left, and the apartment is the bottom right one."

"Ma'am," one officer said, "we need you to come with us and point it out." *No.* I really didn't want to do that. There could be a shoot-out. People could die. *I* could die.

"This way," he said.

I walked with a group of armed guys up a small hill to the back of the apartment building on the right side of the road. The front of that building overlooked my building. We took the stairs up to the second floor and walked through the outdoor hallway to the front of the building so I could point out my apartment—in the open air.

I was thinking, "You've got to be kidding me. He's got guns in that house. He could come out shooting right now. And they all have on bulletproof vests, and I don't have one, and he could come right out and target me and just shoot me in the head."

I stood at the railing pointing now. "Look," I said, "my apartment's right there. The bottom level. 3414. The second one on the right." I was almost leaning over the rail to point through a clump of trees. *Lord, am I going to live through this? What if I don't live through this?*

They led me back down the stairs now, out the back of the building, and down the hill to the bridge area. I saw dozens of guys with rifles and flak jackets and helmets huddling together and getting organized. *Oh, God, don't let it explode around here. Just keep the lid on this thing. Please. Please!*

A big, kind of squared-off black van had pulled up right at the bridge, and the police took me to stand behind it. "Stay here," they said. I just kept thinking, "I'm standing here out in the open? What if he comes down that hill and guns just start going off?"

"Hey," someone else said to me. "Did you know there's a reward out for this guy?" "No," I answered. I was remembering Brian's words: "You'll be on the news."

Right then I could hear shouting: "It's him! It's him!" I looked around the van, and a car was coming down the hill toward us. A black man was behind the wheel. *I already told you guys he didn't have a car. Unless he stole one.*

"Get behind the van!" someone yelled at me. "He might have a gun." I squatted down. *Oh, God, please, no. Don't let this happen.*

Then I heard someone say, "It's not him. Let him go." *Thank you. Stay with me. Don't leave me.*

I started praying like crazy: "Lord, please don't let people die. Don't let him come out shooting. Just let him come out—let him come out without those guns. Let him surrender. Don't let them go in there and kill him. I can't walk into my house and see blood splattered everywhere. If I have to see that ... Just, please. Please."

I was thinking about Brian. My emotions were all over the place. I thought: "Did I betray him by saying he could stay there—I mean,

I didn't want to have to do this. I begged him to turn himself in. I gave him every opportunity." Then: "Ashley, what are you thinking? The guy killed a bunch of people and held a gun in your face. And if it wasn't for God keeping his finger straight like that, he could've just pulled the trigger and you'd be dead." Then: "But I know he was sorry for what he did. I saw that side of him. I don't want them to blow him away in my apartment."

Standing behind the van, I could just picture Brian coming out with a gun and shooting agents everywhere and guns going off all around me. I could almost hear the shots right then. It was like I was just waiting for it all to start. And I didn't want to hear it. I didn't want to have to see it. *God, just help. Help. Help. You've got to do something here. Let him come out. Let him surrender. Don't let anyone get hurt. Do something.*

At some point they moved me into a police car. I was so glad not to be out in the open anymore. Then I thought: "Aunt Kim." I took out my phone and dialed her number. She answered. "I'm in the back of a police car," I said quickly. "Brian Nichols was at my house all night." "What?" "Yeah, he was in my house." I started crying. Tears were coming down my face. And then she was gone. An officer had taken the phone out of my hand.

"Ma'am, we need to talk to you right now."

Now I was sitting in the back of another police car, trying to answer questions about the night and remember what had happened. *Ashley, just think. Think so you can tell them what they need right here.*

Suddenly, as I was talking, an officer said something and turned his head. I looked out the window to my right, trying to see what he was talking about. And right there—right there—was Brian Nichols. Walking down the hill from my building. With his hands behind his back. *He's not shooting. He's just walking. What's happening?* He had my Willie McGee's tee shirt tucked into those khakis that were too short. He wasn't wearing any shoes—just the white socks he had gotten out of my drawer. And he was holding his head up as a blond FBI woman in a navy sweatshirt, with some more guys behind her, led him by the arm.

My mind was racing. "It's over. Is it over? Is he done? I can't believe it. No one's shooting. Oh, God, just thank you—no one got hurt. He's still alive. He made it. He's going now—going to pay for what he did. He didn't lose it. He didn't get those guns. I mean, he completely gave himself up like he said he would."

Then I thought, "What's he feeling right now? God, please forgive him for what he's done. Help him right here. I mean, he listened to me. He listened." *God, you really listened.*

27 walk-through

A couple of days later, I pulled up to my apartment with a group of two lawyers and two police officers—we were doing a walk-through. The apartment had already been searched and cleaned out once by the FBI. But now I was going back with the Gwinnett County Police just to look around and point things out. And I needed some clothes. My mom was going to pack up my stuff and get it moved out in a week or so. She had come to get me at the apartment complex the day Brian surrendered. The fight we had been in before all of this started was over, and she was taking care of me and helping with all of my business. I was moving out after living in this place for just a few days—I could never stay here again—and this was my last trip inside.

The lawyer who was driving me pulled his truck into one of the parking spaces right in front of my door, and already I was having a strange, kind of eerie feeling. It was like the night was happening all over again: I was getting out of the car. I was about to make a run for my front door. Brian was in the truck behind me. Then there was that click. I didn't know how long I could stay inside with these guys right now.

We walked up to the door, and they let me in. I was trying to be matter-of-fact about being here, but just seeing that closet door in front of me and imagining being backed up against it freaked me out. "Please don't kill me!" I was saying to Brian Nichols. "Please don't hurt me!"

"Look," I said to the lawyers, pointing as we stepped into the living room. "The mirror. He hung my mirror."

I couldn't believe it. I mean, it was off center, but he hung it. The hammer and the Tupperware container of nails—that was Mack's container; he kept nails and tacks in these different ones—were sitting out on the coffee table. And so was the level belonging to the agent Brian Nichols had killed.

Right then one of the police went over to the wall and took my mirror down. "Wait," I said. "That's like a four-hundred-dollar mirror—you can't take my mirror." But they took it. *Oh well. Whatever.*

The curtain rod with those tan and cream panels was lying there where I had left it on Paige's toy box. *I guess he wasn't really up for hanging that.* And on the side of the coffee table closest to the door was my empty juice glass and, next to it, my Bible and my book. *Did he ever look at those?* I couldn't tell if they had been moved.

We walked into the bathroom now. The shower curtain was still pulled back a little. I looked in the bathtub, and I saw the FBI had taken *my* washcloth from off the shampoo rack hanging on the showerhead—not Brian's. They had left his. I just kept thinking about blood, and the people he had killed, and just, was there blood on that washcloth in there? I looked away.

The picture of Paige and me at the wedding was still there on the counter next to the sink where I had left it after washing my face that morning. For a minute I could remember sitting on that vanity stool and holding the picture and just crying as I talked to Brian. "I'm not going to make it out of here," I was thinking. "I'm going to die and never see her again. What's she going to feel like? She won't have a mommy or a daddy. She'll just be sad forever."

But I did make it. You got me out of here, God. I still remembered how it felt to be with my little girl that first night back in Augusta after everything was over. Paige and I were sitting on Aunt Kim's sofa with the TV on. I was almost too tired to breathe, and Paige was sitting right up against me. I could barely hold my eyes open, so I just stretched out on the couch and put my head in Paige's lap. She played with my hair and let me lie there. And my heart just about broke.

Standing in the bathroom now, I could remember thinking to myself at some point that morning, after I made it out of the apartment, "God, what did I do to make you save me?" I was like, "I can't believe I really made it." When Brian Nichols first came through that door that night, I thought my life was done. I just knew God was about to take me home. He was taking me home because of my mistakes. That's what I thought. I had made too many mistakes to count, and God was through playing. It was just over.

And then to walk out the door that morning? I knew I might have been the only person Brian Nichols had come into contact with and not killed. He had shot those people at the courthouse, and the agent. He had admitted to me right here in this apartment that he had killed that man. Brian Nichols could have done whatever he wanted to me. But he didn't hurt me. He hardly touched me. I mean, he taped me up. He carried me into this bathroom right here. I put a Band-Aid on his finger at the kitchen sink. But that was about all there was for contact.

And yet, at the beginning he was pointing that gun in my face and all I could think was, "He's going to pull that trigger. He's crazy, and he's about to lose it and pull that trigger. God's taking me home." *Just what did I do, God—to make you save me?*

I glanced over at the bathroom counter again and saw that the last line of ice was gone now. Maybe the FBI got it—I hadn't let law enforcement know about it yet. Maybe Brian did something with it before he surrendered. I didn't know. I was just glad I could stand here with these people and know that I didn't do it. I didn't do those drugs. And God was proud of me for that. Even right now I could feel him smiling down on me and saying, "Good job, Ashley."

We were standing in the bedroom now. That pile of tape and the curtain panel and the extension cord were all gone. *Those guns.* For some reason, I got down on the floor at the end of the bed and lifted up the skirt. I didn't know why. I mean, I knew those guns weren't going to be there. Of course the guns were gone. But I just wanted to look. I was thinking back to that morning: "Is he done—is it over? Are they under here because he's done with this, God?" Now I knew the answer was yes. They were under the bed because he was done.

Just as I was getting up, I saw something on the floor by the nightstand that was nearest my closet. I stepped over there and bent down. It was the small key chain tin I had kept the ice in. *How did it get over here?* I tried to think back. I thought I'd left it with the zipper pouch on the bathroom counter after laying out those lines for Brian. But maybe not.

I could still remember what I was thinking after Brian untied me, and I went for that pink zipper pouch under the fold of my comforter. I stood there at the bed and for the first time ever, I thought to myself, "I would rather die because I didn't do those drugs than die doing them." And then there was what I told Brian in the bathroom before he snorted that first line up his nose. I said, "This is God's way of telling me, 'Look, Ashley, stop now. I'm giving you one more chance. You better stop right now, little girl, or I'm bringing you home. It's your choice.'" *It was my choice.*

Well, it seemed I had to be faced with death to really take a stand for God and say, "This is who I am. I'm choosing God now. I'm through with that other way." I mean, I had been faced with death before—when I got into my car accident, I could've died. And there were those times when I thought, "Whoa, I've done way too many drugs—Lord, please don't take me home yet." But I'd never had death staring me in the eyes like this. Never a gun in my face. And I guessed that was what it took. God finally just had to put his foot down: "I'm here, Ashley. You can stop. You can live for me."

Looking at that tin on the floor now, I thought, "What if it's still got dope in it?" I picked it up right then and stuck it in my pocketbook. I would let the authorities know about the ice soon. I would let them know about it soon.

Walking into the kitchen, I saw Brian's juice glass sitting on the bar near my picture frames. I could still imagine him bending over those tools to look at the photographs. That was when I was standing at the sink washing the breakfast dishes, and I was thinking, "Maybe he just wants some normalcy in his life."

"Let me show you who those people are," I had said to him. And at the time I was remembering what he had said to me at breakfast: "Maybe God led me to you because of the families—to let me know how they felt because you've gone through it yourself."

Looking around the kitchen now, I saw that the breakfast dishes I had washed that morning were still sitting in the drying rack next to the sink. And across the room on the counter by the microwave was the raspberry soda bottle. I could just see Brian coming into that bathroom with that thing and pointing it at me: "Want something to drink?" I was sitting cross-legged in the tub. "Make yourself at home, dude," I was thinking.

Suddenly one of the lawyers turned to me. "You ready?" he asked. "Are you ready to go?"

"Yeah," I said. Yes, I was ready to go. I was starting to feel tired. And kind of freaked out from all of the flashbacks. I needed to leave this place now. Leave it for good.

Walking back around the bar, I thought back for a minute over the whole night—the whole seven hours with Brian Nichols. And what stood out right then as I was adjusting my bag of clothes on my shoulder and getting ready to leave it all behind was just—I don't know—freedom. Somehow, I felt free when I was in here that night. Free to be myself. I really *found* myself in this apartment. I stood up for God and said, "I'm living for you. I don't care if it's popular. It's all about you, God."

And maybe taking a stand like that, making that choice, just set me free. I mean, I was through with the drugs for good—and this time it was solid; I felt that in my heart. I was free to have another chance at life. God *gave* me that chance. I sure didn't deserve it—I'd blown so many others. He gave me my family back; he let me live so I would have another chance to love them right and quit lying to them. He gave me another chance to be Paige's mom. I was amazed, totally amazed by it all. God just had mercy on me.

Really, I didn't even know how I had done what I did—how I got through the night and talked to Brian Nichols so he could see what he needed to do. I only knew that God did it. God was helping me. He gave me things to say and showed me how to open up my life. He worked on Brian so that he could hear what I was telling him. He gave me strength, faith, hope, and love. It was just God—helping me and doing what needed to be done.

"Here take this." I was remembering what Brian said to me as I was trying to get out the door that morning. He was standing near the bar, trying to hand me that forty bucks. He must've known then what he was going to do. I didn't trust him. I thought he might start running. I didn't know why those guns were in there under the bed. But he knew. He really must've known he was done. Now he was paying, and I'd given that forty bucks to the authorities and it was over. I hoped Brian knew he had done the right thing. And that his heavenly Father was pleased with the choice he made to give himself up, to surrender.

"Wait," I said now, as the men were walking out the front door.

I went to the coffee table and got my Bible and my *Purpose-Driven Life*. I wasn't leaving those—no way. I still had another seven or eight days left to do in my book. And I wasn't missing. I wanted to hear every word God was going to say to me now. Every single word. It was like I could just feel his pleasure right then—the way my book said. I could still feel him smiling on me. It was an amazing feeling. Somehow I'd made him proud. And all I cared about as I turned around to leave, all I could say was, just, "God, what can I do to make you smile again?"

epilogue

In the months since being held hostage by Brian Nichols, a great deal in my life has changed. Some days I wake up and think *everything* has changed. My life is by no means perfect, but it is different. In many ways—the most important ways—it finally seems to be on the right track; and for that I am grateful.

Probably the most obvious difference in my life is the publicity that has followed the events of March 12. Within a day of Brian Nichols's surrender, people found ways to contact me with media requests, and later with book offers and movie offers. I never expected the kind of attention I received; I just did what I could to stay alive that night in my apartment, hoping I would get to see my daughter again. Until then, I was a struggling single mom trying to battle drug addiction, regain custody of my child, and put my life back together. I didn't feel prepared for publicity when it came. But I didn't feel prepared for Brian Nichols either, and if God got me through that experience, then he can give me what I need now. I know that sharing my story is important, and my sincere desire is to bring hope to others who need it.

Along with the publicity have come so many gracious demonstrations of support. I've received mail from people all over the world—some letters were addressed simply to "Ashley Smith, Bridgewater Apartments." I've tried to answer many of these letters to show my thankfulness, and I donated the checks I received to my church in Augusta, The

Church at Greenbrier. To those people who have prayed for me, though I may never know you by name, I want to thank you from my heart. God is moving in my life, bringing healing and change; and I know he is moving in response to prayer. I owe you a debt of gratitude.

Another big change in my life is the financial blessing that has resulted from my ordeal. On March 24, in a ceremony at the Georgia capitol, I received reward money from Georgia Governor Sonny Perdue and other officials and was given a chance for a new start. For the first time ever, I can take care of my daughter's material needs, something I never believed I would be able to do without my husband. My twelve-year-old brother, Christian—this year's state gymnastics champion for floor—did a back flip in the governor's office the day I received the reward. He expressed just how I felt inside: grateful, humbled, and blown away by the appreciation of others and the goodness of God to me.

I have tried to be very careful with the money given to me and with the money I have received for writing this book. I've donated some to my church and taken steps to stabilize my finances after years of struggling. I bought a reliable car to replace the old Pontiac Bonneville I was driving when Brian Nichols took me hostage. I also put money toward something very important to Paige.

One day Paige asked me, "Mommy, where are yours and daddy's wedding rings?" I was surprised by the question, and I really didn't want to answer her. The truth was, I had pawned those rings—for less than a hundred dollars—about a year after Mack died. I pawned them to get money for drugs, if I remember correctly. And I pawned them without even caring; that was my state of mind at the time. I didn't want to feel. I didn't care about anything.

When my daughter asked about the rings, I couldn't believe I had let go of something so precious to her without even thinking of her feelings. And even though I had pawned those rings three years ago, I decided I would go back by the pawnshop and just look. "Who knows?" I thought. I didn't really expect anything, but I was curious. It couldn't hurt to look.

So I went. I walked in the shop's front door and went straight to the glass jewelry case. I couldn't believe it. There they were—the rings Mack and I had bought together—almost like they were sitting there waiting on me. I bought those rings back and took them home. And I set them aside for my little girl.

One of the most significant developments in my life since leaving my Duluth apartment March 12 came with a phone call I got one evening in late June. A law enforcement official was on the line, and he told me that two arrests had been made in the stabbing death of my husband. New testimony had been given, I learned, and a grand jury had indicted two men for Mack's murder.

This news was huge for me—just shocking. I don't know what role publicity from the Brian Nichols crisis played in helping the investigation, but the timing made it hard to believe there was no connection. More than anything, getting that phone call brought an overwhelming sense of relief. After nearly four years of my husband's death being unsolved, learning about the arrests has provided some of the closure I've desperately needed. At the very least, the arrests have helped me *begin* the process of closure. Now I know that in time our memory of Mack will become more peaceful. Now I can tell my daughter that progress has been made in the case of her daddy's death and that justice will be served.

Beyond the external changes and developments in my life, it is the changes others might not see that are precious to me. After years of disappointment, personal failure, and strife, my family relationships are being healed in ways difficult to describe. My relationship with my mom grows deeper daily—we have never been as close as we are now. My mom and my Aunt Kim are beginning to trust me. My relationship with Paige is pure and full of love. My entire family is happy that I am whole again and part of them. I pushed them away for so long, and now they have welcomed me back. I am touched, sometimes floored, by their love and acceptance and by the way they have responded to me in the midst of my recent experience.

I still hope to have a career and my own home one day. I also know the time will come for me to regain custody of Paige. For now, though, I am taking things slowly. I am learning how to be a good mom and a confident, stable person. And right now I feel healthier in my emotions than I ever have before—my heart feels healthier. I can love my daughter better. I am learning to guide her, discipline her, and shelter her. I used to be scared to do that on my own; I felt so weak and inadequate. But now I know that I am not on my own. God is with me, and my relationship with Jesus Christ has become the thing I cherish most.

God is helping me in many other deep, important ways right now, too. I am still drug-free—I haven't touched drugs since walking out of my apartment on March 12. Since that day I have continued to cooperate with the investigating authorities. I have let them know about my past and that I had drugs in my apartment that night. Initially I did not volunteer the information about the drugs; when I was first interviewed by law enforcement, I believed their primary focus was Brian Nichols. And I was afraid. Later I came forward and shared the details about the drugs with the appropriate authorities, but I regret not having done so at the very beginning. I remember what Jesus said: "The truth will set you free." That's how I want to live my life—I want to be an honest person and experience the freedom that goes with it.

Meanwhile, I'm trying to do my part to stay clean of the drugs. I am keeping accountability partners and asking for God's guidance. Instead of running away from God's voice, now I seek it and try to learn from his words. I focus on the things I learned at recovery. I do not go to meetings right now because of publicity, but I plan on going and sharing my story of addiction and recovery as soon as I can. I do pray regularly with my pastor. He was the youth minister at the Baptist church I attended growing up, and he has been a very important source of strength for me throughout my ordeal. I take part in a women's Bible study group, too—the prayers, love, and support of these women have provided me with a sense of security I've badly needed.

A year ago I never dreamed I would be surrounded by the kind of strong, healthy, supportive people that God has put in my life; I often think I don't deserve it. But I know that if I'm going to recover and stabilize my life for good, then I need solid people around me. I still pray all the time for the friends I knew in the drug scene. While it isn't healthy for me to be with them right now, these people have good hearts and many God-given talents—they just can't see through the fog of the drugs. I want these friends to make it out of all that, and I pray that what has happened in my life will impact them in some way. I want them to know that God loves them no matter what they've done. I want them to know God's forgiveness and that it's never too late for God to turn a life around. He's the God of the second, third, fourth, and fifth chance; he never gives up on anyone. If he can change me—the one they called "Crazy Girl"—then he can do anything!

On a recent night in July, I was flying back into Atlanta from Denver, where I attended a book convention. I had gone to the convention to promote this book and to share some of my story with the people there—it was my first time getting up in front of an audience and giving what some might call a speech. (I called it my testimony.) I remember being so nervous before I stood up that when I got to the podium and noticed how dim the room looked, I felt grateful. At least I didn't have to see the people's faces!

Everyone was so good to me at the convention, so supportive and complimentary. But it still felt awkward to be praised for what happened with Brian Nichols—to be called a "hero." Since the events in March, I had never been comfortable with that word. I wrestled over it. And I just kept saying to people at the convention, "God's the one who did it. He helped me. I don't want to take the credit."

Flying into Atlanta now in the dark, I could see a sprawl of lights twinkling underneath us, and for a moment I thought back to March 11, the day Brian Nichols was on the loose. Three people had been shot at the courthouse, and later the agent at his house. Others had been injured, some carjacked. Lives were turned upside down. The whole city was on lockdown. As I looked at the lights on the ground, I thought, "So many of the people in those houses down there were scared on that day. And all I had to do when my time came was be faithful and obedient to what God was telling me. And because I did that, those people didn't have to be scared anymore."

That was a pretty overwhelming thought—that something I did had helped others on such a large scale. And yet, like I told those people at the book convention, I knew it was God. He helped me to make good decisions that night; I couldn't have done what I did without him. God was the real hero. Yes, I did something. I played my part. But it was a small part in the grand scheme of things.

There are so many others who played their parts. There are the countless people who prayed all night for Brian Nichols's capture and for the safety of the city. Those prayers helped me while I was awake for those seven hours talking to Brian Nichols and hoping I could convince him to do the right thing.

And if there are any heroes, they are the judicial and law enforcement officials who risked and gave their lives trying to bring the crisis to an end. I only saw those officers, agents, and officials who gathered in droves at Bridgewater Apartments the morning of March 12. But there are so many others—people I will never know—and I honor them.

Most importantly, there are the three men and the woman who died on March 11: Judge Rowland Barnes, court reporter Julie Ann Brandau, Deputy Sergeant Hoyt Teasley, and Special Agent David Wilhelm.

They are the heroes in the story.

While I was with Brian Nichols, I knew very little about what had happened those hours he was on the loose. I only knew that there were victims. But now I know more. I know more about these four dedicated public servants, their lives, and the impact they had on others. I am privileged to share a little about each one of them in the tribute that follows.

I also know more about the loved ones these four victims left behind. On some level, I can imagine their suffering because of my own experience; and in just imagining it, my heart breaks for them.

To you who have survived the loss of your dear one—husband, wife, father, mother, brother, sister, aunt, uncle, grandparent, child, friend—I extend my deepest sympathies and my prayers. I know the pain of losing someone precious to a violent murder. It is an indescribable pain. It runs deep. And so many questions go with it. It is so difficult to understand why our loved one died and why this is happening. My prayer for you right now is that God will be with you in a powerful way and give you the strength, support, courage, and hope that you need.

To Deputy Cynthia Hall, who has had to fight for her life, and now her health, after being severely injured in the assault by Brian Nichols, my prayers are with you and your loved ones as you recover. May God give you strength, faith, and hope right now—may he meet all of your needs.

To those who were attacked or carjacked by Brian Nichols on that day—Almeta Kilgo, Deronta Franklin, Don O'Briant, and others shaken or injured after crossing his path—my prayers are with you. And with all of those people tied to the terrifying events of March 11: those who have suffered and feared, those who have gone back to work at the courthouse, those who in any way were affected by the events and have kept on. I thank you for your example and your courage. May God be your strength and your help.

All of you are heroes to me.

a tribute to the victims

I was a very fortunate survivor in this tragedy with Brian Nichols, but these four public servants were not. They each gave the ultimate sacrifice, and they leave behind loving friends and family who must go on with their lives. I do not understand why some are taken and others are spared. I am so humbled and blessed to be alive, and my hope is that my story will bring some comfort and peace. I am honored to devote some of the royalties I earn from this book to create a memorial that will serve as a permanent tribute to the victims.

Superior Court Judge Rowland W. Barnes, 64, was serving his seventh year on the Fulton County bench at the time of his murder. He died in his courtroom shortly before the Brian Nichols trial was scheduled to begin. Widely regarded as one of the most beloved figures in county government, Barnes was often described as jovial, fair, and warmhearted. A graduate of Emory University Law School in Atlanta and a native of Wyoming, Judge Barnes left behind a loving wife, Claudia, two daughters, and four stepchildren. His daughter Kiley, 26, plans to become a lawyer and continue her father's legacy.

Court reporter Julie Ann Brandau, 46, was a dedicated "Guardian of the Record," the title court reporters across the nation sometimes give themselves as they work long hours to transcribe everything said in a courtroom. However, she always found time to bake pound cakes, peach bread, or cookies for juries during trials. A native of Moncks Corner, South Carolina, and the youngest of three girls, Brandau had been the court reporter for Judge Barnes since 1998, when he was appointed to the bench; she had worked for more than twenty years in the Fulton County courts. Loved by colleagues and friends alike, she and her college-age daughter, Christina, enjoyed travel and took trips to Hawaii and Costa Rica.

Deputy Sergeant Hoyt—known to family and friends as Keith—-Teasley, 43, was recognized, even as a boy, for his protective instinct. He once went off on his bike to help search for a missing neighbor; and when a firecracker exploded at a family gathering, he threw himself over his sister to cover her. Teasley also was considered a great neighbor—a friendly and quiet person who would offer to help others with their yard work. An Atlanta native, Teasley served with the Georgia Air National Guard, and he joined the Fulton County Sheriff's Department in 1986. He is survived by his wife, Deborah, and his young daughters, DeKeisha and Deona.

U.S. Immigration and Customs Enforcement Special Agent David Wilhelm, 40, had served in federal law enforcement for eighteen years. His friends and family remember him as a strong leader, smart, honest, and hardworking, and as someone who loved and could connect with people. He also had a talent for home building and remodeling—he was laying tile at his new Atlanta house the night he was murdered. Born in Salisbury, North Carolina, Wilhelm had been transferred to Atlanta in late 2004 to continue a career as a rising star. He left behind a beloved wife, Candee.

acknowledgments

First, I would like to thank my Lord and Savior Jesus Christ. If he did not love me as much as he does and have a plan for my life, then I would not be alive to share my story through this book.

I want to thank my daughter Paige for loving me no matter what and for being one of the best prayer warriors I could ever ask for. You are my heart and I love you so much.

I would like to thank my mom for demanding that I go to Bridges of Hope and for saving my life after my car accident. And for all the love and belief she has always had in me. Thank you, Mom, for putting up with me and never giving up on me. I love you, and I promise I am here for you every step of the way as you fight this battle with cancer.

Larry—aka "Dad"—thank you for treating me like your own and for always loving me. Thank you for showing love to Mack when he was alive and for helping him to see what he wanted in life. Thank you for never giving up on me and for being there when many would have written me off.

I would like to thank Aunt Kim for all of the love and support she has given to me and to Paige. Thank you for all of your prayers. Thank you for challenging me to want more of what Christ has for me. Thank you also for your guidance and friendship. And Uncle Steve, thank you for being the best father figure that Paige could ask for and also for your love and open arms to me.

I honor and thank my grandparents for always guiding me in the way of the Lord and for loving me when I did not seem to love back. Mema, thank you for showing me the person I want to be—just like you! And Papa, thank you for instilling in me the discipline I have today. I know it comes from you, and I would not be the same without it. I told you guys I would make you proud someday!

To my Uncle David ("Uncle D") for the talks we have had, for the prayers you have prayed, and for the example you have set for me as a godly man, husband, father, and friend. I hope there is one more man left out there just like you for me. Aunt Jill, I want to thank you also for your prayers and for all the time you spent with me when I was growing up. Those times are memorable.

To my brother Christian and my sister Leah—thank you for loving me. Christian, I am proud to be your Sissy, and Leah (aka "La"), I am proud to be your Sisso. I love you both with all my heart.

To my "cuz" and best friend in the whole world, Rebekah: thank you for all your love, support, and prayer, and for being hard on me when you needed to. It's okay—I forgive you, and I hope you forgive me too! Thank you also for checking my email and being my "assistant" through everything. I will have you home soon. And Eric too—thanks! I love y'all.

To all the rest of my family, thank you all for your love and support and, most of all, for your prayers. Jesus heard you when you prayed, and he answered. I love you all—you guys are the best family anyone could ever ask for!

To the Smith family, thank you all for loving Paige and me. Thank you for your love, support, and prayers. I know that Mack is at peace now.

Thanks to William Davis and Son for giving me a job when I first moved to Atlanta.

To all of you at Jackson Spalding, thank you for caring about me and loving me the way you do. Thank you for making my dreams come true. I couldn't have done this without you. You guys are my "new friends" the Lord has sent. Glen Jackson, thank you for always standing firm for Jesus Christ and knowing where my story needed to be. Thank you also for making me feel less afraid the first night we met—I will never forget your prayer. Caroline Duffy, thank you for becoming full-time again because of me. You have been my ears when I couldn't hear, my eyes when I couldn't see, and my voice when I couldn't find the words. I am grateful, and I love you. Thanks to Stephanie Fitzsimmons, Gustavo Machado, and Tony Wilbert for your professional support as well.

To my agent, Calvin Edwards, thank you for your faithfulness, all of your hard work, and for spoiling me with the many gifts you sent! You and Nerida have been wonderful to me. I know God sent you to me from the very beginning. And Heather Northcutt, thank you for the help you have provided.

To my lawyer and friend David Nutter, thank you for your guidance and for the talks that we have had about our heavenly Father. You too were God-sent, and I appreciate everything you do.

To my CPA, Courtnay Bazemore, thank you for all of your hard work and for being the best woman for the job. You have been God-sent as well.

Thanks to Josh Archer for giving up part of his weekend and dropping everything on his plate the week of March 13 to run interference for me. I am grateful you were there to lean on.

To the people of Atlanta—thank you for the gracious way you have supported me since the terrifying events of March 11 and 12. I mourn with you for the loss of those who died; our city is less than what it was because they are gone. A special, heartfelt thanks to Governor Sonny Perdue and the other officials who honored me on March 24 and extended a reward to me. I appreciate your support and am humbled by it.

To those everywhere who prayed for Brian Nichols's surrender and a peaceful end to the violence, thank you from my heart. God answered your prayers, and I am grateful.

To Zondervan and William Morrow: thank you all for believing in me and my story, and thank you for helping me make my dreams come true. Thank you for your hard work, generosity, enthusiasm, and kindness. I appreciate you more than you know.

On the Zondervan side, I want to thank Executive Editor John Sloan for your guidance and belief in my story, and for all of the stories you have shared with me—they have changed my life. My thanks also to Jim Ruark, Senior Editor; Vicki Cessna, Director of Public Relations; Mark Rice, Vice President of Corporate Communications; Lyn Cryderman, Vice President and Publisher, Books; Scott Bolinder, Executive Vice President and Publisher; Bruce Ryskamp, Chief Executive Officer. A special thanks to audio producer Jeff Bowden for his work with me on the audio book.

On the William Morrow side, I want to thank Executive Editor Maureen O'Brien for your strong belief in this story from the beginning, all your editorial guidance, and your energy and openness with me. You have been so fun to chat with, and you have put so much into this book. I also thank Stephanie Fraser, Maureen's excellent editorial assistant; Debbie Stier, Director of Publicity; Trina Rice, Publicist; Lisa Gallagher, Publisher; Michael Morrison, President; and Jane Friedman, Chief Executive Officer. A special thanks to Associate General Counsel Beth Silfin for all of her input and hard work.

To my dear friend and pastor, Chuck Gordon, thank you for The Church at Greenbrier—I feel so at home there. Thank you for your concern and for all your prayers and support.

To Dr. Frank Page, thank you for all your support and prayers, and for letting people know during the beginning of all this that I am a child of God and have been for a long time. I just got lost, and Jesus is the one who found me.

To my Aunt Kim's prayer group—thank you. You guys have always known that prayers get answered, and now so do I.

I also want to thank my small group for all of the fellowship and for your constant prayers for me over the last six months. And to everyone who has begun to pray for my mom and her battle with cancer, thank you so much. We need you. Please keep praying!

To Bridges of Hope, thank you for showing me the way of hope and for teaching me that I am an addict. Thank you for giving me the knowledge to recover and stay recovered. To all the recovering drug addicts out there, just knowing you're out there trying to stay clean one day at a time keeps me encouraged! To the drug addicts not yet recovered, thank you for showing me where I came from—but please know there is a better way, and it is Jesus.

To the Columbia County Sheriff's Department, thank you for your work on Mack's case and for doing your job and never giving up. And to the Honorable Judge Duncan Wheale, thank you for your guidance and concern for Paige and me.

Last, but so importantly, Stacy Mattingly, thank you first for being so Christlike. Thank you for your prayers and concerns. Thank you for being able to "become me" and do this book the way Jesus wanted us to. We did it and I know he is smiling! You are a great friend to me. I know who to call when I need a prayer, and that is one of the best feelings in the world.